Jacob Kornbeck

Inspiration from Brussels?
The European Union and Sport

Selected Willy Calewaert Lectures (2010–11)

AF061365

EHV

Kornbeck, Jacob

Inspiration from Brussels? The European Union and Sport
Selected Willy Calewaert Lectures (2010-11)

ISBN/EAN: 978-3-86741-864-5

First published in 2013 by Europaeischer Hochschulverlag GmbH & Co KG, Bremen, Germany.

© Europaeischer Hochschulverlag GmbH & Co KG, Fahrenheitstr. 1, D-28359 Bremen (www.eh-verlag.de). All rights reserved.

Brussels Sprouts Football Pitch
Cover design by Les Années Lumière, Brussels; cover foto: Eric Hunt – Idea © Jacob Kornbeck 2013

No part of this publication may be reproduced or transmitted, in any form or by any means, electronic, mechanical, photocopying, recording or otherwise, or stored in any retrieval system of any nature, without the written permission of the copyright holder and the publisher, application for which shall be made to the publisher.

Jacob Kornbeck

**Inspiration from Brussels?
The European Union and Sport**

Table of Contents

Prologue 9

Chapter 1 Not only Regulation, but also Inspiration from Brussels: EU involvement in sport matters – an opportunity for renewal in the sport sector? 12

    1.1. Introduction: inspiration versus regulation 12
    1.2. Voices from practice 14
    1.3. Inspiration "from Brussels" 17
    1.4. Diversity as an opportunity for mutual learning 25
    1.5. Conclusion: unprejudiced inspiration; applying the principles of free-mindedness 26

Chapter 2 The Fight against Doping between Efficiency and Proportionality: a role for action taken at EU level? 29

    2.1. Introduction 29
        2.1.1. Objectives of this chapter 29
        2.1.2. The inherent contradictions of the fight against doping 30
    2.2. Examples of action taken by the various EU Institutions 35
        2.2.1. The Council (cases 1-2) 35
        2.2.2. The European Parliament (case 3) 36
        2.2.3. The Court of Justice (case 4) 39
        2.2.4. The European Commission (cases 5-9) 43
        2.2.5. What do the seven cases show us? 50
    2.3. What the EU can do 54
        2.3.1. Providing more fairness to competitive athletes 54
        2.3.2. Promoting the sharing of information and good practice 55
        2.3.2. Regulating and harmonising? 57
        2.3.3. General conclusion 59

Chapter 3 Play, Not Therapy: the EU's role in promoting health-enhancing physical activity (HEPA) 61

    3.1. Introduction 61
    3.2. Introducing overweight, obesity and physical inactivity 62
        3.2.1. From societal problems to policy challenges 62
        3.2.2. What can (and should) the EU do? 66
    3.3. Challenges to academic disciplines and to the professions: physiological, medical, social science, social work, education and PE perspectives compared 75
        3.3.1. Physiological and medical perspectives challenged by critical social science and social work perspectives 76
        3.3.2. Critical social science and social work perspectives and their limitations 80
        3.3.3. Sport and physical activity as a supplement and an alternative? 82

- 3.4. What role for the sport and physical activity sector? 83
- 3.5. From analysis to action: taking stock of the potential role of the EU 86
  - 3.5.1. Possibilities for political cooperation 86
  - 3.5.2. Possibilities for incentive measures (funding) 97
- 3.6. Conclusions 100

Epilogue 102

References 105

- European Commission (Sport Unit) documentation 105
- Literature 105

Willy Calewaert (1916–1993)
(VUB archives collection)

Prologue

> „Der Unterschied liegt auf der Hand: gesprochene Worte eines Mannes in brauner Kutte mit gefalteten Händen gegenüber anonymen Internet-Teilnehmern, die die Informationen in Sekundenbruchteilen auf den virtuellen Weg schicken. Aber die Gemeinsamkeiten sind auch nicht fern: Traditionelle und Zukunftskräfte haben beide vielfach die Möglichkeit zur Kommunikation und den Wunsch, die Gemeinsamkeiten über das Trennende zu stellen, vereint auch zu handeln."
>
> *(Herrmann, 2009, p. 2)*

Based at the Dutch-speaking Free University of Brussels (*Vrije Universiteit Brussel*) (VUB), the Willy Calewaert Visiting Chair is an endowment of the relatives of the late Willy Calewaert (1916-1993), former law professor and Belgian Minister of Education (1973-4, 1980-1) and the Civil Service (1979-80).[1] For the academic year 2010-11, this Visiting Chair was assigned to the undersigned to teach a range of lectures within the thematic area of the European Union's involvement in sport policy matters.

In line with the VUB's philosophy of unbiased thinking – including the legacy of Willy Calewaert,[2] of the VUB and of its French-speaking sister university (*Université Libre de Bruxelles*) (ULB) – I took this as an opportunity to reflect without bias on policies related to the sport sector. This seemed to be of particular pertinence and salience given that this sector, in many (if not most) of the Member States of the European Union, presents itself as being discreet and distinct from other walks of life. This "specificity" (an English neologism often used on debates on the EU's impact on sport) is usually underpinned by long-standing arrangements between public authorities and civil society organisations in the field of sport, to the extent that sport's claims to "specificity" are largely supported by public authorities, be it explicitly or implicitly. Because the EU does not have any stakes in such age-old arrangements, it has the opportunity to take a fresh, unbiased look at many issues. This was the basic philosophy followed in accepting the Visiting

---

[1] For a short biography, see:
http://www.vub.ac.be/vlaamsestudenteninbrussel/personen/willycalewaert.html
[2] The emphasis is here on unbiased "free thinking", rather than on specific issues. The author does not share the late Willy Calewaert's approach to abortion but his insistence on free thinking, which may indeed lead to dissimilar outcomes, depending upon the evidence examined and values and methods employed in assessing the evidence.

Chair for the academic year 2010-11. Readers will find a more detailed exploration hereof in Chapter 1 of this book.

The assignment would appear to represent a specific wish, on the part of those responsible for taking the decision, to have the 2010-11 lectures taught by a professional rather than an academic, as my employment is with the European Commission as a civil servant in the role of a Policy Officer. The texts included in this publication should be understood from this aspect. Again, these ideas are explored in Chapter 1, including by drawing on academic and literary concepts of the "reflective practitioner."

Lectures delivered by the Chair holder included an introduction to the topic "the EU and sport" (Chapter 1), the fight against doping (Chapter 2) and health-enhancing physical activity (Chapter 3) as well as thoughts on likely future developments in the wake of the implementation of the Lisbon Treaty. Of these four lectures, the latter was not included in this book, granted that recent developments have taken place at an impressive speed, potentially necessitating totally reworking this text (whereas the book aims at ensuring publication of the three previous texts before they will have become partly obsolete as a result of intermittent policy developments). Readers will thus find a general exploration of the topic together with two substantial case studies.

As a matter of intellectual honesty, I preferred desisting from giving certain lectures, the topics of which would lie outside of my areas of expertise. Instead, with the blessing of the VUB, acting on behalf of the Calewaert family and the union of free-thinking associations (UVV), I invited two Commission colleagues, Gianluca Monte and Bart Ooijen, to teach the lectures for which I did not regard myself as being competent. In the aftermath of the lecture cycle, a book publication has been planned which will include two strongly edited chapters based on two of the lectures given by me (doping, HEPA) (see below), chapters based on lectures given by Gianluca Monte and Bart Ooijen as well as chapters written, for that particular book, by VUB staff and other academics.[3] In an effort to make the original versions of my own lectures available to a wider public, this publication has been prepared to include the inaugural lecture as well as the full-length version of two further lectures (doping, HEPA). The concluding lecture was not included as it would have needed substantial editing to take subsequent policy developments into account.

---

[3] Theeboom, M., et al. (forthcoming): EU Involvement in Sport: between inspiration and regulation. Brussels: Academic & Scientific Publishers (ASP)

Thanks are owed to the the relatives of the late Willy Calewaert, the VUB and the UVV for having rendered the lectures possible. The author would also like to thank Professor Marc Theeboom and Mrs Helena Wittock (VUB), as well as Professor Hans Westerbeek (Victoria University, Institute of Sport, Exercise and Active Living (SEAL), Melbourne, Victoria) for cooperation before, during and after the lectures. Thanks are also owed to my colleagues Gianluca Monte and Bart Ooijen for their contribution.

Disclaimer

The author is a civil servant in the European Commission (Policy Officer in the Sport Unit) but opinions expressed in this book are those of its author and do not render official positions of the Commission.

Chapter 1
Not only Regulation, but also Inspiration from Brussels:
EU involvement in sport matters – an opportunity for renewal in the sport sector?

> *"Les idées ne sont pas faites pour être pensées mais pour être vécues."*
>
> (André Malraux) (1901-1976)

1.1. Introduction: inspiration versus regulation

This chapter aims to introduce the subsequent chapters which are all based on lectures held, during the academic year 2010-2011, at the Free University Brussels (*Vrije Universiteit Brussel, VUB*) as part of the annual, inter-faculty Willy Calewaert Chair. The introduction will set out the rationale of the lectures, which is also that of the book. Under the title "Inspiration from Brussels," the lectures asked what EU involvement in sport matters means in terms of providing the sport sector with alternative insights and ideas for their future work. By referring to *inspiration*, the book aims to provide an alternative to the image of "Brussels" – a convenient, yet largely reductionistic metonym for the European Union (EU) (the way "Hollywood" is used to allude to the US film industry) – as the source of *regulation* only, i.e., of binding rules, the application of which is regularly resented.

As an alternative to this – widespread yet partly erroneous – representation of "Brussels", the book will show that not only regulation, but also inspiration can come "from Brussels": EU involvement in sport matters is not only a source of announce for some, but also an opportunity for renewal in the sport sector. By way of an example, the well-known Bosman ruling of the European Court of Justice (ECJ) may, in 1995, have come as a surprise to many functionaries in sports organisations, whose reactions were far from favourable as it led to a reshuffle of the transfer system in professional football. The impact of the Bosman case has been judged to be so paradigmatic, by the editors of a major academic publication dedicated to the development of ECJ case law during its first half century (1960-2010) (Poiares Maduro & Azoulai, 2010), that it is one of just twelve landmark ruling selected for inclusion in what aims to illustrate the development of case law in diachronic perspective. Each of these twelche rulings has been discussed by four specialist authors, and one of them is Bosman: at the time of publication, a case that was actually 15 years old.

If proof is needed that sport is an important facet of European integration – and such proof may be demanded, given that sport is still absent from most text books, be it of European integration (in political science textbooks) or EU law (in legal textbooks) – the place of prominence occupied by the ruling in this publication (Poiares Maduro & Azoulai, 2010) must have proven it, or at least it must have made it emerge as extremely plausible. Between the 1962 Van Gend en Loos ruling, establishing the supremacy of EC law over national law (a principle that has made the EC/EU fundamentally different from forms of cooperation between states hitherto seen), and the 1995 Bosman ruling lie 28 years; it is remarkable that this history finishes, provisionally, with a sport-related ruling. Yet it is equally important that Bosman may be interpreted not only as *regulation*, but also as *inspiration*. Bosman may be seen as the gensis of EU sports law (Van den Bogaert, 2010) and the case that "changed everything" (Weatherill, 2010). For the governing bodies of professional football it was annoying (Parensen, 1998) and continues to be so (Infantino & Mavroidis, 2010)

For players, it meant more freedom, as citizens and as workers; it certainly showed an alternative path for the future and, as professional football has rather been thriving than withering away since 1995, the way it showed turned out to be a liveable (and even a rather profitable) one. For sure, "Brussels" (which in this case should rather be labelled "Luxembourg", since the capital of the Grand-Duchy is the seat of the ECJ, while the Commission is based in the Belgian capital) intervened as a *regulator* of the sport sector; yet in retrospective, "Brussels" has also acted as an *inspirator*, if a slight neologism can be forgiven here. This may seem bewildering to many observers, but as the subject-matter field of sport unfolds: –

- as a subject within the political dynamics of European integration; as a nascent quasi-policy field ("quasi" because EU policies, strictly speaking, are those where formal regulation is possible);
- certainly (and indeed increasingly) as a subject-matter field within the EU institutional system – it shows an inherent mixture of "direct" and "indirect" initiatives (Tokarski & Steinbach, 2001; Tokarski, et al., 2004, 2009);

it: –

- combines "vertical" and "horizontal" features, in that it shows cross-cutting traits (being embedded in various policy fields and various political and administrative structures) while also developing into a field of its own (Kornbeck, 2006b);

- while the developments observed fit well with established "governance" debates which explicitly recognise that governmental actors can take action, not only based on their regulatory roles, but indeed also via networking strategies which are open to private actors also (Kornbeck, 2006a).

1.2. Voices from practice

This chapter was preceded by a quotation from André Malraux. Notwithstanding recent revelations regarding Malraux's relationship with objective reality (Todd, 2005), the basic contention of this book is that its subject matter deserves to be looked at from a practice perspective. The following chapters are the contributions of practitioners rather than of full-time researchers; they provide assessments based on personal experience, of case-handling and of engagement with the subject matter. Far from being a compilation of merely descriptive field reports, the book includes analyses and reflections following the paradigmatic rationale of the "reflective practitioner": the emanation of one particular ideal of professionalism and partly the negation of the ideal of an unengaged professional, as espoused in the 1950s to 1980s.

For while early models of professionalism and professionalisation had emphasised the combination of academic knowledge and practical tasks (Flexner, [1915] 2001), at first without questioning professional rationality (Carr-Saunders & Wilson, 1933), schools of thought following after 1968 emphasised the self-interested ambitions of the professions (Johnson, 1972), or the empirical reality of an emerging "formalised knowledge" (Freidson, 1986) as well as attempts to synthesise between these two strands (Abbott, 1988). Nevertheles, despite the impressive succession of sociological models of professionalisation, it does not seem feasible to deduct any clear single model of professional rationality from them, so that the *reflective practitioner* model proposed by Donald A. Schön (1930-1997), in the framework of professional education (for future teachers) seems more rewarding. Widely embraced in the fields of education and social welfare, this model recognises that action taken in professional practice is not merely the result of a quasi-scientific assessment, but rather the result of a variety of impulses:

> "The practitioner allows himself to experience surprise, puzzlement, or confusion in a situation which he finds uncertain or unique. He reflects on the phenomenon before him, and on the prior understandings which have been implicit in his behaviour. He carries out an experiment which serves

to generate both a new understanding of the phenomenon and a change in the situation." (Schön, 1983, p. 68; cit. Smith, 2001)

Action is taken as needed, in direct opposition to research situations where initiative follows the needs of knowledge generation, as far as possible, often in the framework of a previously defined research design.

> "We have to take certain things as read. We have to fall back on routines in which previous thought and sentiment has been sedimented. It is here that the full importance of reflection-on-action becomes revealed. As we think and act, questions arise that cannot be answered in the present. The space afforded by recording, supervision and conversation with our peers allows us to approach these. Reflection requires space in the present and the promise of space in the future." (Smith, 1994, p. 150; cit. Smith, 2001)

On the empirical level, there would appear to no direct contradiction between Flexner's six traits of professionalism (indeed a mix of rational and less rational, ideal and pragmatic values and imperatives), on the one hand, and Schön's "reflective practitioner" on the other. Rather, the professional ideals flowing from these two different models are necessarily dissimilar, one being rooted in a conception of the professional as a distant expert (Flexner), the other being fully aware of, condoning and even supporting the embedded role of the professional into his or her working environment.

Thus, while the "Schönian" ideal of professionalism may appear as being in stark contrast to the "Flexnerian" ideal, in that it deliberately renounces some of the (essentially academic) distance between the professional and the subject matter assessed for action to be taken), the same contradiction cannot be said to exist between "Schönian" ideal of professionalism and the "Humboldtian" ideal of academia, whereby it is submitted that European academia is still, by and large, following Wilhelm von Humboldt's (1767-1835) ideal of the combined teacher-researcher (Kornbeck, 2007). A dilemma (denoting a contradiction which is problematic) can be expected to be found between the "Flexnerian" professional and the "Humboldtian" academic (in that both lay claims to a certain degree of objectivity), but not necessarily between the "Schönian" professional and the "Humboldtian" academic, between whom the division of tasks if clearer. Instead of a dilemma, the apparent contradiction would be an antinomy (a system of opposites which is necessary and unavoidable, as it is constitutive; hence it should be seen as an opportunity rather than as a problem). In this perspective, "voices from practice" become a useful addition and complement to the analysis provided by the members of academia themselves. This is the spirit in which the following chapters should be read.

The distance usually preferred in academia has here given way to a perspective which recognises the embeddedness of the observer within the context of observation; the nearness of engaging with the subject matter; and a focus on authenticity and relevance for action. Such assessments should be of interest to the employees or elected leaders of sports organisations or civil society in general, teachers, health professionals, social workers and social pedagogues, but also government employees, consultants, etc. It is hoped that they will also be of interest to academics, as a supplement to academic analyses which, in this field, are rather sparse anyway. Indeed, there is no inherent contradiction between professional knowledge and academic knowledge: they are complementary rather than contradictory. The European university is an old invention, the first ones having been founded in the 11th century and although universities occasionally see themselves accused of reflecting in an academic ivory tower, there is nothing in the concept of the university that obliges us to do so, just like the accusation is far from always supported by evidence. Universities are wonderful places to discuss public policy – not only the policy of government, but the politics of society at large, including civil society – and practitioners can make a different kind of contribution in this regard, bringing in their field experience.

In the 1952 Spring semester, Russian novelist Vladimir Nabokov (1899-1977) held a series of lectures at Harvard about Cervantes's Don Quijote – in English known as Don Quixote (hence the adjective "quixotic" to denote an effort that is based on more determination and than calculation). Nabokov was not a scholar but a novelist, yet his lectures (Nabokov, 1984) show a profound knowledge of this work of narration, no doubt based on an intensive perusion of it. Where a full-time academic would have kept a certain distance to the subject matter, Nabokov submerges himself in it. Where a full-time academic might have spent a considerable amount of time comparing variegating positions taken by other scholars, Nabokov goes for one type of reading, but his interpretation is convincing and forceful due to its internal coherence and the detailed knowledge of the novel about the Manchegan squire. And should these considerations seem rather far away from our subject matter, the EU and sport, readers are invited to read Nabokov's analysis of Don Quijote's victories and defeats, drawing on the rules of the tennis game. Despite this being an anachronism (modern lawn tennis having emerged after Cervantes wrote his novel), Nabokov forcefully demonstrates that the sequence of fights and brawls in which Don Quijote (deliberately, as a rule) gets involved corresponds with a series of tennis matches, each subdivided into sets. If we use the rules of tennis – a tribute to the *homo ludens* rationale of sport – we end up with the astonishing result that Don Quijote and the aggregated totality of adversaries are at equality at the end of the book: the score is 20-20 (Nabokov, 1984, pp. 97, 104, 110) – what a wonderful tribute to the inner wisdom of sport! But the analysis is that of a full-time novelist, not of a full-time researcher. It is hoped that something similar can be said about the subsequent chapters.

1.3. Inspiration "from Brussels"

An introduction to this book would be incomplete, were it not address the last unusual phrase found in its phase: for what exatly does inspiration "from Brussels" imply? As stated above, "Brussels" is the handy-yet-reductionistic metonym used by the domestic press, media and decision makers in the Member States of the European Union to refer to decisions taken and developments taking place at EU level. For many other Europeans, "Brussels" is a distant entity, and more often than not, the reference to the mysterious entity "Brussels" implies some kind of action taken by remote control, possibly also "by stealth" ("Brussels has decided", "Brussels says we must", "Brussels says we can't"...). While it is to be admitted that a convenient shorthand can be needed when reporting about complex matters developing in an institutional framework with often long and cumbersome names and acronyms – e.g., the European Council (Heads of State and Government, the Council of the European Union (Council of Ministers, half of the EU legislature) and the Council of Europe (another governmental organisation, based in Strasbourg and not part of the EU framework) are all different despite the strikingly similar names – the reductionist approach chosen by many commentators may often actually increase the confusion. For decades, the French press and media have been referring to the European Commission as *la Commission de Bruxelles*, yet this being an entirely home-made name which can be found in no official text, it may actually make it more difficult for citizens to track a news story down to the relevant documents, starting with the official EU websites, where the fantasy name is absent for the very good reason that it only exists in French press articles and TV programmes.

Against this backdrop, readers may legitimately ask what sense it makes for a publication like this one to use the "Brussels" label in an equally home-made fashion, especially in the adverbial form beginning with "from": does not the phrase "from Brussels" have a ring far too familiar and consonant with more or less populistic news stories? The basic submission of this book is that the phrase may have such a ring, yet it does deserve being used a catchy, yet precise *Leitmotiv*. For the ambition, in using this title, is precisely to challenge the taken-for-granted and the conventional wisdom about the EU and, thereby, to make it plausible that inspiration may come "from Brussels" just as well as regulation. Furthermore, the book intends to show that inspiration *and* regulation often come in a tandem, although not exactly hand in hand. Yet to fully appreciate the significance of this proposed new strand of thought – not totally unfamiliar to the model of Multi-Level Governance (MLG) (see e.g. Rosamond, 2000) – it is necessary to summarise what is special about the EU and the regulatory powers it actually does hold (and does wield) in some fields: that the field of sport is most often not one with much regulatory power makes it, if not an exception, then at least a specific case study in its kind.

It is hardly surprising that it should be easy to portray "Brussels" as a mega bureaucracy, more the size of the US federal administration, given that even citizen-friendly, rights-based initiatives of the EU can easily be attacked, in the national press and media, as encroaching upon national rights; as an example out of many may be quoted a German press article on EU legislation aimed to prevent discrimination in the workplace (Merkur, 2008). Assuming a community of interests between national authorities and citizens which cannot always be confirmed by objective facts, such mechanisms remain powerful, yet as a Dutch academic, writing for the benefit of NGO's, points out "Brussels" is actually "an exceptionally small bureaucracy", suffering from endemic "volume and content overload" (van Schendelen, 2006, p. 66) precisely due to its resources which are extremely limited and the ensuing "overload" (ibid., pp. 66, 84, 114, 257, 275, 293, 294). "EU myths", including big bureaucracy, centralism, formal powers and always assuming real influence, elitism, democratic deficit as facts rather than attempting to prove them by means of evidence are therefore a fact of life that needs to be counted on in discourses involving the EU Institutions.

While "Brussels" may, therefore, often be something of a misnomer (not so much because Brussels is not the actually location of decision-making, but rather because power lies more in the national capitals than in Brussels), it also glosses over the fact that different EU Institutions have different roles and responsibilities. While it should be recalled that legislative power is closely limited by the narrow confines of the principle of conferral (power is held to the extent that it has been conferred by the Treaty), the possibilities to take action in specific cases varies from one EU Institution to another, with legislative power being held by the Council and European Parliament in conjunction, legislative power by the Commission and judicial review being carried out by the Court (General Court, ECJ, Civil Service Tribunal) and the

Committees (Economic and Social Committee, Committee of the Regions) holding consultative roles only. This means that the public is not always presented with initiatives of a legally binding nature, although news coverage may often provide this impression.

- In the area of sport, enforceable EU secondary law (*acquis communautaire*) applies, as can be seen in the fields of free movement relative to players' right to take employment in other Member States (the ECJ's Bosman ruling 1995); Internal Market and competition law relative to the marketing of TV transmission rights (the ECJ's QC Leisure ruling 2011); or data protection law relative to procedures and practices in anti-doping and athletes' individual rights as data subjects (the on-going controversy since c. 2008). Such developments can rightly be said to represent *regulation* "from Brussels".

- Yet other means of influencing developments in this sector exists, such as communication via the EU Sport Forum, with a growing and increasingly diverse array of participating organisations, as compared with its beginnings in 1991; incentive measures (funding) for a variety of network projects, not only from sport-specific budget lines but also from EU programmes without a sport focus (Public Health, Citizenship, regional funds, etc.); or social dialogue at EU level (which does become binding for its signatories once signed). Finally, the Eu can play an important clearing-house role, as exemplified by the few yet very influential special Eurobarometer surveys dedicated to sport and physical activity, which have led to thought-provoking academic research (cf., Scheerder & Van Tuyckom, 2007). Rather than regulation such developments are examples of *inspiration* "from Brussels".

The European Union and its predecessors, the European Communities (ECSC, EEC, EAEC, EC), are unique in having seen a transfer of real governmental sovereignty to a supranational level (unlike international governmental organisations such as the UN, Council of Europe, etc.), yet they did so without setting up a new super-state (as was the case with Wilhelmine Germany). This means that sovereignty is vested in the EU, and that the EU can take legislative, administrative and judiciary action just like any national government can on its territory, yet only in certain well-defined areas of so-called "exclusive competence". It also means that new, supranational challenges arise (Herrmann, 2009, p. 84). But the "supranational impetus" is not always as strong as some would expect (be it because they support or because they oppose stronger integration): social policy is another illustration of this principle, backed by the relevant Treaty provisions (ibid., p. 25). The fact that the EU sometimes really acts as if it were a state, while in many (most) other cases it cannot and does not, presents a bewildering picture to even more seasoned observers. The fact that flexing its regulatory muscle can have great impact (recent high-profile anti-trust cases make this abundantly clear) obscures the fact that its budgetary means are extremely limited, as are the financial contributions of its Member States; its administration is negligible and easily dwarfed by those of big cities in Member States, yet the impression of an almighty European superstate prevails, helped by sensationalist elements in the press and media, and often by domestic decision makers eager to blame "Brussels" for unpopular measures. According to Herrmann (2009, p. 234) (again writing on social policy, albeit with obvious implications for sport policy) this mechanism can be especially reinforced by the subsidiarity principle.

Without going into too much detail regarding each school of thought, its basic premises and main contributions, it should be note that the tension between European (supranational) and the national level, between interpretations of institutional arrangements which emphasise the powers transferred to the European level, on the one hand, and positions which claim continued responsibility and agency for the national level, seems to go like a read thread, not only through European integration itself (the empirical phenomena observed) but indeed also through the academic (sub-)discipline of European integration (the discourse addressing the observations made). In this context, we shall limit our remarks to the observation that the federalism of the 1950s-1960s emphasised (and advocated) formal transfer of power to the European level (Mitrany, Monnet, etc.); that it was challenged by various later schools, including the (liberal) intergovernmentalism of the 1980s-1990s (Moravcsik); that a more pragmatic, empirical perspective had already been adopted in the 1950s-1970s by the so-called functionalists, whose interest was with function more than with form (Haas, Lindberg); finally, that a wide array of pragmatic, integrating approaches emerged in the 1990s among which Multi-Level Governance (MLG), based upon the empirical observation of the structural funds and the direct interaction they allowed between the European and regional level, without any formal amendments having been made as regards the EU-Member State relationship (Marks & Hooge, etc.). (For a discussion of theories of European integration, see e.g. Rosamond (2000); for a discussion of how to apply these theories to the subject matter "EU & Sport", see Groll, Gütt & Mittag (2008) or Mittag & Groll (2010).)

This has special ramifications in the case of sport, given that this sector already enjoys a special status of more or less developed autonomy from governmental regulation in many Member States (while often drawing on important governmental or para-governmental source of funding and support): whereas the EU is unconditionally subsidiary to Member States in this field (see Article 165 TFEU) (*Treaty on the Functioning of the European Union*) (see further below in the same section), it is equally true that, in many Member States, national authorities are actually subsidiary to sports organisations. The established theories and models of European integration need, therefore, to be applied *mutatis mutandis*. Research on the "EU & Sport" topic is still underdeveloped yet nascent. (For an overview, see Groll, Gütt & Mittag, 2008; Mittag & Groll, 2010; Tokarski & Steinbach, 2001; Tokarski, et al., 2004, 2009.)

As the EC/EU did not have an explicit, Treaty-based mandate for sport for a long time – only with the entry into force of the Lisbon Treaty (1 December 2009) was a sport provision included in the Treaty (Article 165 TFEU) – the development of the file "EU & Sport" became a matter of political initiative (as far as the socio-cultural aspects were concerned) and ECJ case law (as regards the regulation of professional sports). While the new provision does not change any of the existing *acquis communautaire* (be it on free moevement, media rights, data protection, etc.), a will to develop the non-regulatory, non-economic aspects has manifested itself since the early 1990s, including via the defunct Eurathlon programme (for details, see Tokarski, et al. 2004, pp. 64-65), the European Year of Education through Sport (EYES) 2004 or the increasing EU involvement in matters related to obesity prevention. Education and training represents an area where, despite the absence of regulatory powers, the driving interest is at least as much socio-economic as it is socio-cultural. (For an exemplary overview of developments in higher education, see Petry, et al., 2008.) The continued existence of a socio-economic "market coalition" and an alternative "socio-cultural coalition", both trying to influence the course of events at EU level, observed almost a decade ago by Parrish (2003, pp. 65, 161, et al.), means that stakeholders have partly contradictory expectations regarding what the EU should do.; whether the EU is empowered to take actions as invited to, is obviously another matter. (For a discussion of these coalitions, drawing on the conceptual model of advocacy coalition, see García García, 2007, 2008.)

The combination of a Treaty competence without "hard law"; very limited ressources (especially human ressources); dissimilar expectations among stakeholders; and a pressure to take some sort of action have all made consultations crucial, including the annual EU Sport Forum (since 1991) and a series of ad-hoc on-line consultations. As such, the field of sport is not an exception or a case apart, as consultations are now an established element of EU governance (Herrmann, 2009), yet this field remains a more outspoken case for making extended use of consultations.

All such expectations must be read in the light of Article 165 TFEU which grants the Union a mandate to act only in a supporting, coordinating and supplementing role, to:

> "contribute to the promotion of European sporting issues, while taking account of the specific nature of sport, its structures based on voluntary activity and its social and educational function." (Article 165 (1) TFEU)

In terms of objectives, provision is made for EU action to target

> "developing the European dimension in sport, by promoting fairness and openness in sporting competitions and cooperation between bodies responsible for sports, and by protecting the physical and moral integrity of sportsmen and sportswomen, especially the youngest sportsmen and sportswomen." (Article 165 (2) TFEU)

While the exact meaning of this provision remains to be clarified, the reference to "the physical and moral integrity of sportsmen and sportswomen" is remarkably direct, semantically suggesting protection not only against doping and overtraining, but also against verbal and physical (possibly including sexual) abuse).

To achieve the objectives set, the EU and its Member States may

> "foster cooperation with third countries and the competent international organisations in the field of education and sport, in particular the Council of Europe." (Article 165 (3) TFEU)

Observers not versed in the technicalities of EU law may be forgiven for reading these provisions as a strong mandate for the EU to take pro-active measures with profound and unavoidable consequences for the established decision makers of the sport sector (Member States, sport organisations), yet the devil is the detail. For not only is Article 165 TFEU based merely on an EU "competence to carry out actions to support, coordinate or supplement the actions of the Member States" within the meaning of Article 2 (4) TFEU; it is listed as one of the areas covered by such a competence (the least powerful of three different levels of EU competence) in Article 6 (e); the impossibility to harmonise the laws and regulations of Member States is further pointed out in Article 165 (4) (although it would not have been strictly necessary, given the structure of the Treaty and the way in which general provisions impinge upon special provisions); finally, the formal actions which can be taken in pursuance of Article 165 are listed once again as incentive measures (funding) adopted by the European Parliament and the Council, "acting in accordance with the ordinary legislative procedure, after consulting the Economic and Social Committee and the Committee of the Regions, shall adopt incentive measures" and Council recommendations "on a proposal from the Commission" (Article 165 (4) TFEU).

From this prescription, it will be seen that the article is not first and foremost about the legal aspects of the organisation and governance of sport. Some might have hoped it would be, just like some thought the 2007 White Paper should have served to cement certain special arrangements in the field of sport; some sports organisations with a high level of professionalisation and important commercial interests had hoped and expected that the White Paper (and later the Treaty article) would have served to grant blanket exemptions from rules otherwise applied to businesses "Much work remains to be done," was the conclusion of a joint IOC & FIFA statement (FIFA, 2007). A "Missed Opportunity" was the verdict of A. Brown (2007) in the World Sports Law Report; one wonders just who had missed an opportunity. And yet – like the Court did in 1995 when it decided about the transfer of Jean-Marc Bosman[4] – the Commission was not even proposing to create new law, rather providing a snap-shot of the existing situation. Yet it is important to note that sports organisations of this type have one sort of concerns, while those of sport-for-all organisations are rather different. For the International Sport and Culture Association (ISCA), an umbrella organisation representing sport-for-all organisations, the priority is rather to ensure sufficient means for grassroots sports and to raise participation levels for the entire population, not to avoid free movement and anti-trust law (see ISCA, 2011), and certainly not to have intellectual property rights (IPR's) and TV transmission rights protected to their advantage: different organisations see different types of ghosts and have different expectations regarding the role played by the EU Institutions.

Notwithstanding the variegating (and partly contradictory) expectations and messages from sport stakeholders, Article 165 is the text, and this text is the law. Important parts of the *acquis communautaire* continue to be applicable to athletes and sports organisations: free movement, anti-trust, but also labour law and data protection. Against this backdrop, therefore, high

---

[4] This is the opinion of many legal experts (see Ilešič, 2010; Van den Bogaert, 2010), even if it is rejected by some other authors, who may be closer to certain sports organisations (see e.g., Infantino & Mavroidis, 2010).

expectations have to be revised and fears of regulation have to be moderated; yet there is ample margin for many forms of inspiration "from Brussels".

Inevitably, the perspective of the subsequent chapters tends to be that of the Commission – a natural reflection of the authors' own professional role, although the chapters were written in a personal capacity and, as such, do not render Commission positions – and the extent to which Commission action can be said to represent *regulation* or *inspiration*, or possible a combination of both, will regularly take a central position, while fully recognising the role played by other EU Institutions as appropriate. In fact, the most discussed Commission initiatives tend to be Communications and White Papers, which are never binding as such, although they may include proposals for binding measures. In the field of sport, these include proposals to follow up on the legacy of the European Year of Education through Sport (EYES) 2004 (European Commission, 2005); in the 2007 White Paper, a variety of proposals on how to use the pre-Lisbon legal and political framework to take initiatives in a wide range of areas (European Commission, 2007); and the Commission's proposals for the implementation of the new post-Lisbon framework in the field of sport (European Commission, 2011).

Within the pre-Lisbon framework, an inventory approach, seeking for creative solutions based on existing, limited tools, seemed well advised: in relation to the use of sport and physical activity to enhance health and counteract, for instance, a wide array of instruments could already then be identified (Kornbeck, 2009). In a post-Lisbon perspective, this might change again, depending on the legal and material nature of each single file; the criminal law harmonisation of the fight against trade in illicit doping substances could, for instance, profit from new instruments in the field of criminal law (Kornbeck, 2009). While the EYES Communication contained no proposals for legal action, the White Papers opened up this possibility, in principle, in relation to players' agents; on trade in illicit doping substances it supported Member States' on-going criminalisation efforts, and this message was well received in the national press of some countries where it served as inspiration, including Denmark (Aagaard, 2007). Finally, in the 2011 Communication, this line of thought was taken further, still without proposing an actual EU Directive; yet the mixture of regulation and inspiration continues to be in a "10:90" rather than in a "50:50" ratio. Yet even without legal action being taken, the EU is expected to use the post-Lisbon framework to contribute to developments and debates affecting the sport sector. When the Council adopted its European Union Work Plan for

Sport for 2011-2014, it entrusted an EU Expert Group Anti-Doping with preparing an EU contribution to the review of the World Anti-Doping Code (WADC) (Council of the European Union, 2011). If the EU manages to have some of its more radical proposals accepted by the other stakeholders if the World Anti-Doping Agency (WADA), this would certainly be a prime example of inspiration "from Brussels": it would not have been imposed, but nevertheless accepted due to the cogence of its arguments and the validity of the material quoted. Given that the current WADC contains numerous contradictions and inconsistencies (Kornbeck, 2011), the WADC review is certainly an interesting candidate in this respect; success in having key amendments made would be a major case for claiming the relevance of *inspiration*, as opposed to *regulation*, "from Brussels":

1.4. Diversity as an opportunity for mutual learning

Chapters will show readers different mixtures of regulation and inspiration. In any event, they will make it apparent that being a Member States of the European Union provides opportunities for mutual learning, whereby not only differences but indeed also commonalities should come to the fore, be it as part of non-binding political cooperation with Member States, the so-called structured dialogue with sports organisations or multi-actors networks supported via EU funding programmes and allowing a multitude of constellations regarding the participating organisations and the activities concerned.

Mutual learning often leads to the realisation that not only content, but also concepts, vary, as a study of Chinese sport shows, due to the absence of the European body-mind dualism, a paradigm rooted in Greek phiosophy and handed down to the present idea via the Christian tradition: in stark contrast herewith, Chinese sport concepts were always holistic and the health-enhacning functioning was never seen as different from the ludic one (Klöpsch, Lämmer & Tokarski, 2008, p. 5). In Europe, sports plays have for centuries been seen as a category apart (Huizinga, [1938] 1962, p. 13), based on the assumption that "sporting movements" know no ends because they are an end in themselves (*die Zweckfreiheit der sportlichen Bewegung*) (Grupe, 1984, p. 87): that sports organisations should claim exceptionalism and "specificity", not only for their purely sporting activities but also for other activities of theirs, is hardly surprising. Yet the Chinese example shows that alternatives exist – despite the obvious European success in exporting the concept of Olympianism to the rest of the globe (Höfer, 2008) – and begs the question to what extent European societies actually do share the same sporting concepts. Indeed, even democracy (a concept often seen as common to all of Europe) varies greatly, both as regards how it is structured, how it is understood and what are the standards to measure it by. One sport scholar has likened the three main types of European democracy to three main forms of sport: Anglo-Saxon absolute majoity voting in single-candidate constituencies (such as the British First-Behind-The-Pole system) then corresponds to team sports where one must win and the other must lose, the efforts of the latter having been wasted; proportionality as practised in many Continental and Nordic systems, where every efforts counts something, is likened to track and field, with its obsession with accurate measurements; participative democracy, finally, comes closest to the German and Nordic gymnastics (*Turnen*) movement, where all are involved, noone wins and noone loses (Eichberg, 2004).

Despite the limtations such a comparison covers, due to its level of abstraction, it nevertheless does provide a powerful illustration of diversity and a reminder than neither sport, nor democratic governance, are exactly the same across Europe (cf., Jesse & Fischer, 2010). Some may actually see a particular sport as an emanation of a particular national culture, e.g., Jahn's gymnastics as "a singularly Germanic activity" (Hardman, 2002, p. 1). Should this appear too disturbing in times when the cross-border level-playing field is increasingly claimed in the interest of "sport", it should still be remembered that Europe remains the most diverse of the globe's continents, relative to its very limited size (König, 1993, p. 17): diversity applies to most aspects of life. Although the exchange of information and good practice does not automatically lead to innovation, as the external evaluation of certain, recent preparatory actions in the field of sport has revealed (Economisti Associati, et al., 2011, p. 40) (certain conceptual and structural criteria need to be met to ensure effectiveness; efficiency and added value), there nevertheless is a very strong case for reflection and action testing how to make the most of these instruments.

1.5. Conclusion: unprejudiced inspiration; applying the principles of free-mindedness

If free-mindedness is not simply to mean anticlericalism (as it has too often done in given political situations in Belgium),[5] but indeed an open mindset which applies the same rigout to all social phenomena, then it seems

---

[5] Note that the author is a Christian committed to free thinking and rejects dogmas, including possible dogmatic paradigms based on the rejection of other people's spiritual and/or religious perspectives.

particular promising to apply to the world of sports the same critical attitude which has, for a long time, been applied in this part of Europe to the Catholic Church. In the summer of 2011, Germany's Federal Labour Tribunal took many observers by surprise when it confirmed the decades-old privilege of Germany's recognised Churches (Catholic as well as Protestant) to dismiss their staff on the ground of conduct in their private lives. Specifically, and in direct contradiction with normal labour law standards, a Catholic hospital had the right to dismiss a physician for having remarried after his divorce (Die Zeit, 2011a): an exceptionalism which bears strong resemblance with the so-called "specificity" of sports organisations and their demands for exemptions. In the case of the Catholic Church, the extremely favourable treatment received by German judges suddenly looked very odd when, during his visit to Germany in September 2011, Pope Benedict XVI called for all such privileges to end and for the Church to submit itself to the authority of the state (Die Zeit, 2011b); the critical observer might then wonder in whose name German judges were upholding this doctrine of specificity.[6] German trade unions did not agree with this legal doctrine, insisting that Protestant church employees should be entitled to strike (Kamann, 2011).

Yet sport organisations continued – and continue in many cases – to claim such exceptionalism. Clearly, the sport sector continues to perceive itself as fundamentally different from the mainstream of society, to the point of questioning the legitimacy of rules adopted by democratic states. While exceptions may be made on a case-by-case basis, there is a need for communication on the importance of extending, as far as possible, the same rights and obligations to all natural persons and legal entities within the same jurisdiction. If indeed the Catholic Church is more prepared to accept the authority of the state than the sport movement is, then there is a clear case for free-mindedness in its most fundamental sense: for unprejudiced scrutiny of the state of the art, and for free reflection on possible alternatives. This is what this book aims to illustrate, via a selection of case studies, as did the lectures which were held at the VUB.

---

[6] Note that recognition of religion and spirituality does not depend on their embeddedness or not in the structures of recognised religions; see the "spiritual-but-not-religious" debate in social work (Wong & Vinsky, 2009) and the debate on a *spiritualité laïque*. Note also that the German controversy on the application of labour law standards is by no means limited to the Catholic Church (as some might possibly assume if looking at it from a Belgian *laïc/vrijzinnig* perspective): in November 2011, employees of Germany's Protestant churches were protesting against a rule banning them from striking; they were supported by Ver.di, a mainstream trade union (Kamann, 2011). (Compare this to the late and slow, yet nascent unionisation in European professional league football and basketball.)

It seems fair to assume that the EU Institutions may provide inspiration by way of alternative ideas, given that national, regional and local authorities often have their established networks with sports organisations. That the EU cannot host the Olympics and does not have a national team may be deplored by some; here it should rather be seen as an opportunity. The submission is that the very diverse actions taken by actors at EU level, as set out in the following chapters.

Chapter 2
The Fight against Doping between Efficiency and Proportionality: a role for action taken at EU level?

"À force de lire on finit par comprendre qu'à force de lire on finit par comprendre."

(Jacques Beaudry)[7]

2.1. Introduction

2.1.1. Objectives of this chapter

What contribution can the European Union make to the fight against doping? The subject matter of this chapter is potentially a vast one, if one were to seek answers as to how the EU could reinforce the fight across the board, and yet, most of the answers found would inevitably prove impractical due to the absence of a corresponding EU competence under the terms of the Treaty. For while Article 165 TFEU (Treaty on the Functioning of the European Union) does include a reference to the fight against doping, it explicitly rules out harmonisation and implicitly excludes all other legally binding measures, due to the competence for sport being one to "carry out actions to support, coordinate or supplement the actions of Member States" within the meaning of Article 6 TFEU.

Against this backdrop, the chapter will show how the EU has, until now, contributed to the fight in a few selected areas; the list is not exhaustive, neither will the chapter deal with all potential possibilities, granted that some already enforceable EU legislation might possibly be relevant to anti-doping activities and could in some cases support it (Röthel, 2000; Vermeersch, 2006). After a discussion of the inherent contradictions of the fight, and why they make it problematic for all public authorities to commit themselves too strongly to supporting it unconditionally (section 2.1.2), examples will be provided of how the major EU Institutions have been dealing with anti-doping matters: the Council and the European Parliament essentially by adopting non-binding measures (section 2.2.1-2.2.2); the Court of Justice by adjudicating certain cases on the basis of enforceable (but not directly doping-related) EU law (section 2.2.3); and the European Commission sometimes on the basis of "hard law", as guardian of the Treaties, but other times on a "soft law" basis using various forms of

---

[7] Quoted from: La Libre Belgique, 13 November 2012

cooperation (section 2.2.4); finally, the chapter will show how EU funding may make a contribution to anti-doping activities (section 2.2.5).

This material will reveal an EU role which is sometimes akin to "regulation" and other times (indeed, more often than not) representative of "inspiration". The chapter will also show how action taken at EU level has contributed to providing more fairness to competitive athletes (section 2.3.1) or the sharing of knowledge and good practice (section 2.3.2), while a purely regulatory or even harmonising role has until now been extremely limited (section 2.3.3).

2.1.2. The inherent contradictions of the fight against doping

In the field of anti-doping, this would inevitably create a permanent problem (apart from the obvious problems located at the level of EU law), as this sector is marked by increasingly high expectations. The autumn of 2010 saw the sudden dismissal of the chief executives of national anti-doping agencies not only in Denmark, but also in Germany; while in Denmark, the chairman of the board was criticised publicly for having taken this step single-handedly (DR Sporten, 2010), German commentators concentrated on the fact that this high-profile, private-law but essentially publicly-funded agency had lost three chief executives in just three years (Teuffel, 2010); for countries of this calibre, these developments should be seen as rather unusual. The most obvious contemporaneous parallel would perhaps be the dismissal in 2009, in the UK, of the chief executive of the General Social Care Council (GSCC), the body responsible for registering the social work and social care workforce, for managing disciplinary procedures on charges of malpractice and for excluding professionals; despite high expectations from politicians, the press/media and the public, the dismissed chief executive was found to have been too harsh (Lombard, 2009). Such charges are not unknown in and around anti-doping, yet the basic mechanism continues to be an individualisation of the problem and, not seldom, a suggestion that individual positive cases point to deviance and moral weakness in the individual athlete, rather than possible faults in the system of competitive sports itself (Vest Christiansen, 2006); as the Pechstein case in Germany has shown, even when guilt cannot be proven according to the agreed standards, athletes are not simply acquitted but publicly alluded to as being guilty in principle (Focus, 2009), and when they avail themselves of procedural rules which are open to them (an essential element of the rule of law), this may be portrayed as illegitimate (Voigt, 2010).

Therefore, any public authority stepping in to further this fight is bound to get trapped in contradictions between the stated need for a credible deterrent effect, on the one hand, and the overarching legal principles and civic liberties of an open, democratic society ruled by law, on the other (cf., Cohen, 2009; Dikic, et al., 2011; Fertel, 2007; Figura, 2009; Hanstad & Loland, 2009; Houlihan, 2006; Krüger, 2008; López, 2012; Waddington, 2010). In a non-authoritarian state, it is a problem if unconvicted athletes are subject to a tighter system of surveillance than convicted paedophiles (Waddington, 2010, pp. 258-259); yet if public authorities commit themselves to the a continuous intensification of the fight, they may find themselves unable to deliver due to legal and moral constraints. On top of this, the EU is greatly limited in its potential to act by the so-called principle of conferral which means that action can only be taken when and as allowed by virtue of a mandate granted by Member States to the Union in a Treaty article.

The fight against doping is hyper-complex and presents decision makers with hard choices, while intensive news coverage puts them under pressure to demonstrate credible commitments. Though undesirable, doping is a natural (side-)effect of competitive sports, possibly a "technology" responding to the need for hierarchy, performance and victory (López, 2012). Despite recurrent claims that doping violates the "spirit of sport" – next to the ban on performance enhancement and the concern for athletes' health, this is the third reason foreseen, in the World Anti-Doping Code, for including a substance or training method on the Prohibited List – it may be asserted, on the contrary, performance enhancement "is not against the spirit of sport; it is the spirit of sport" (Savulescu, Foddy & Clayton, 2004). While arguments may be found to challenge those arguing in favour of legalisation (including health risks, corruption, public safety, etc.), the traditional anti-doping system, as has been handed down to us, is based on bans which involve many contradictions (Møller, 2009). Whether the "spirit of sport" is a Calvinist construct (Overman, 2011), or whether it is deconstructed by social scientists according to other parameters, this concept remains central, not only to the ideology of the anti-doping system, but indeed to the rules which are enforced every day in the world of sports: as such, it is a social fact, relevant in itself. While anti-doping presents itself to the outside world almost exclusively in terms of positivistic science, with an aura of inevitability, it involves political choices, scientific insecurity and even a dose of arbitrariness; yet it is a political and social force and thus an illustration of the "Thomas theorem": that "if men [sic] define situations as real, they. Are real in their consequences" (Thomas & Thomas, 1928, p. 572; cit. Merton, 1995, p. 380)

The anti-doping system is torn between the values of efficiency (essentially the ability to deliver a credible deterrent effect, possibly also the need to show that "something" is being done, and that performance enhancement is not being tolerated, despite its obvious congeniality with the competitive nature of elite sports, for which anti-doping was invented) and proportionality (fairness, the rule of law, refraining from over-zealous measures, respect for the presumption of innocence, etc.). In such a context, clearly, an unbiased outsider with no interests at stake may make a contribution of a different kind; the European Union is such an outsider, being unable to host the Olympics and having no national teams to defend. At the same time, the way anti-doping is dealt with by the Member States of the EU shows a remarkable diversity, as can be seen from the variance in national arrangements regarding athletes' requirements to provide so-called "whereabouts" information allowing them to be tracked for testing purposes (*Table 2.1*). It is not an area in which the EU has any primary responsibility for policies or practices, yet it is one where the EU Institutions are occasionally called upon to intervene, and indeed one where the unbiased look of an outsider may sometimes be beneficial, more often in the form of "inspiration" than in the shape of "regulation", although the latter does play a role in relation to certain aspects of the fight. Yet the chapter will not only discuss how the EU may contribute to increasing the effectiveness of the fight, but also (and especially) how "inspiration from Brussels" (see Chapter 1) may serve as an occasional corrective in relation to this difficult fight, where the efficiency constantly has to be balanced and checked against the usual rules and customs of an open, democratic, free society governed by the rule of law.

The fight against doping may be well-known as a topic in the daily news, and indeed, since the 1990s there seems to have been a consensus regarding the need to pursue this fight more energetically than it was done in previous decades (Krüger, 2008). Although the responsibility of the fight lies with sports organisations and Member States (in various combinations), including national anti-doping organisations (NADO's) (which in turn can be organised very differently, be it under public or private law), the relevance of the EU in relation to the fight has been underlined in recent years by a range of anti-doping related initiatives taken at EU level, albeit by different actors. The Cases 1-9 listed below are grouped according to the four main EU Institutions defined in Article 13 TEU (Treaty on European Union) (besides the European Central Bank and the Court of Auditors). The logic of starting with the Council (while the TEU starts with the Parliament) reflects the fact that Member States remain the de-facto owners of the Union (despite representation of the people within the European Parliament), and also the fact that Article 165 TFEU gives the most pro-active role to the Council. In the field of sport, the Court has often given the impulse for new developments, while anti-doping has only very recently come into the centre of its activities. The Commission has been involved in various ways, not only as guardian of the Treaties but also in amore general role, while the Budget (granted by the Council and Parliament and executed by the Commission) offers potential new possibilities to contribute to the fight against doping, thereby also suggesting alternative directions and priorities. In a policy area where no binding EU initiatives are possible, this is of the utmost importance.

Table 2.1

Country	RTP size[8]	NTP size[9]	Population[10]
Austria	+/- 350	+/- 500	8.3
Belgium (Flemish Community)	682		6.6[11]
Bulgaria	n/a[12]		7.6
Czech Republic	450		10.5
Cyprus	n/a[13]		0.8
Germany	+/- 500	+/- 1,200	82
Denmark	+/- 65		5.5
Estonia	133		1.3
Finland	64		5.3
France	402[14]		64.3
Greece	300		11.2
Hungary	480		10.0
Ireland	230		4.5
Italy	1,500 +		60.0
Latvia	129		2.3
Lithuania	250		3.3
Luxembourg	+/- 34		0.5
Malta	n/a[15]		0.4
Netherlands	+/- 450		16.4
Poland	n/a[16]		38.1
Portugal	+/- 500		10.6
Slovakia	+/- 870		5.4
Slovenia	44		2.0
Spain	274		45.8
Sweden	96	432[17]	9.2
United Kingdom	500		61.7

---

[8] T.M.C. Asser Instituut (2010, pp. 29-30)
[9] T.M.C. Asser Instituut (2010, pp. 29-30)
[10] http://europa.eu/abc/european_countries/eu_members/index_en.htm (visited 29.11.2010)
[11] Including Flemish Region and Flemish-speaking residents of Brussels: estimated on the basis of official population statistics by region of residence, http://statbel.fgov.be/fr/statistiques/chiffres/population/structure/residence/index.jsp, as well as other types of information (6.1 + 0.5 = 6.6) (Lamfalussy, 2010; HLN, 2010).
[12] No explanation provided.
[13] No explanation provided.
[14] Including 143 professionals.
[15] RTP: has not yet been established, hence no athletes are included.
[16] RTP: has not yet been established, hence no athletes are included.
[17] And 106 teams.

2.2. Examples of action taken by the various EU Institutions

2.2.1. The Council (cases 1-2)

Case 1: Council Conclusions and Council Resolutions: This first case concerns texts which are non-binding in legal nature; although they are published in the "C" (communications) part of the Official Journal, rather than in the "L" (legislation) part, they nevertheless enjoy a very high status of so-called "soft law".

The Council [of Ministers] of the European Union is the upper house of the EU legislature and the territorial representation chamber, where Member States meet in national delegations, in opposition to the directly elected European Parliament. Council structures include working groups composed of Member States' experts (in this case the Sport Working Party), the Comittee of Permanent Representatives (COREPER I, COREPER II) composed of Member States' Permanent Representatives (ambassadors) to the EU and, finally, the Council in session (here, the Council of Education, Culture, Youth and Sport Ministers (EYCS)). Despite the supranational character of the EU and the strong similarities between the workings of the Commission, Parliament and Court of Justice with corresponding national institutions of the Member States, the Council has retained many characteristics of classic, intergovernmental structures. (However, this should in no way lead us to see the workings of the Council as proof that the other EU Institutions are less supranational; indeed, the upper houses of Germany and Austria are organised largely along the same lines.)

In the field of sport, the Council is very important. Under the pre-Lisbon framework, it was the Institution where many issues could be taken up, based on other EU competences than sport (which at that time did not exist), while under the post-Lisbon framework, it has been the place where many initiatives have started. This reflects the role of the Council as defined in Article 165 TFEU: that Member States actually have established an EU competence for sport (a policy area closely linked to national identities) may in part be explained by the fact that, by placing the Council centre-stage, they have somehow mitigated the effects of this competence transfer; the European Parliament is needed for allocating appropriate credits in the Budget (but does so jointly with the Council).

Long ago, the Council adopted Conclusions and Resolutions on doping-related matters, including the adoption of a non-binding Code of Conduct in view of the Olympics Games of Barcelona (Summer 1992) and Albertville (Winter 1992) (Council of the European Communities, 1990, 1992). The impact of these initiatives cannot be ascertained, but due to their non-binding nature and the fact that they do not seem to be widely known today, it seems fair to assume that it has been limited. Yet non-binding texts may, under certain circumstances, actually have an impact if they serve as a catalyser of political unity, even in an area where Member States have retained the full power and right of initiative. Thus, the EU was actively involved in creating the World Anti-Doping Agency (WADA), after the European Council (Heads of State and Government), meeting in Vienna in December 1998, had shown its concern over the Festina Scandal of the Tour de France of that year and called for action (European Council, 1998). The principles for EU representation in WADA's Foundation Board were defined in Council Conclusions which were later quoted in more recent Council texts (Council of the European Union, 2000, 2010, 2011b). That the exact formula for EU representation was later to be changed (when the Commission made its seat avilable) is less important for the sake of the argument made here: that Council Conclusions, in spite of their non-binding nature, have proven an effective instrument for fostering unity among EU Member States. More recently, Council Conclusions have been used to launch of a procedure for preparing an EU contribution to the review of the 2009 World Anti-Doping Code (Council of the European Union, 2011a). (Note that the list of Council texts related to WADA is not exhaustive.)

Case 2: EU Presidency initiatives: Reference has already been made to the European Council (Heads of State and Government), which is different from the Council and does not hold legislative powers. Another structure which must be mentioned within this section devoted to the Council and its structures is the rotating EU Presidency. The Member State holding the six-month Presidency may take certain initiatives and give increased visibility to issues, not only via its formal, agenda-setting role (every Presidency defines its Presidency objectives and priorities), but also via punctual actions. In relation to the fight against doping, a study on the "implementation of the WADA Code in the European Union" was commissioned by the Belgian EU Presidency should be mentioned (T.M.C. Asser Instituut, 2010): an example of an informal use of Presidency structures (technically a national initiative) intended to further knowledge-sharing.

2.2.2. The European Parliament (case 3)

As the lower house of the legislature of the European Union, the directly elected European Parliament is made up of Members (MEP's) who organise themselves in factions (according to ideologies) just like MP's do in national parliaments: this contrasts with the logic of delegations (according to nationalities) employed in the Council. Accordingly, the internal dynamics of the European Parliament are not fundamentally different from those found in national parliaments. Apart from forming one-half of the budgetary authority (the other being the Council), the Parliament chamber offers the same opportunities for open debate, often incepted by individual MEP's, just like in national parliaments.

Case 3: Parliamentary questions: In relation to the fight against doping, Parliament has issued opinions on the Commission's various Communications and also adopted other texts, included a Resolution calling for EU-level actions in a wide range of fields (European Parliament, 2005). Questions have been taken up spontaneously, and sometimes in accordance with the priorities of individual MEP's, including the Commission's reasons for not wishing to propose the creation of a European Anti-Doping Agency (Mavrommatis, 2008) or, more recently, athletes' fundamental rights and how these have been affected by the "whereabouts" rules of the 2009 World Anti-Doping Code, be it in general terms (Belet, 2009a, 2009b) or, more specifically, under EU working time rules (Bozkurt, 2008).

> "[...] In hoeverre vindt de Commissie de maatregelen die sporters verplichten 365 dagen per jaar, op elk uur van de dag beschikbaar te zijn voor controles proportioneel ten opzichte van het recht van individuele sporters op privacy? [...]" (Bozkurt, 2008)

The Agency question (Mavrommatis, 2008) pointed to a wish, among some MEP's, to see the EU playing direct a role in reinforcing and coordination anti-doping activities, including by financing part of it, in line with a Parliament Resolution adopted three years earlier (European Parliament, 2005) calling for action in a variety of fields. The questions and answers on working time, related to Article 7 (annual leave) of Directive 2003/88/EC, were gratefully posted, on their website, by an athletes' trade union.[18] The other, more general, question on WADA's "whereabouts" rules stands out as taking a principled and very fundamental position with regards to athletes' fundamental rights, in contrast with the habitual way, within the sports world, of taking exceptions from these rights as a natural part of the sector. The question voices an indignation which is not found in many mainstream sports policy texts:

---

[18] In 2012, the link was found not to function anymore.

> "In België is er heel wat consternatie ontstaan omdat tennisspelers vanwege het niet correct invullen van hun whereabouts voor 1 jaar geschorst werden.
>
> Het nakomen van de whereabouts verplichtingen is sowieso al een ingrijpende maatregel voor 'onschuldige' atleten en roept heel wat vragen op inzake mogelijke inbreuken op de privacy van de atleten.
>
> De veroordeling van atleten in de vorm van een schorsing van 1 jaar voor het gebrekkig invullen van de whereabouts beantwoordt geenszins aan het proportionaliteitsbeginsel, vermits het gaat om atleten die op generlei wijze hun toevlucht tot doping hebben genomen.
>
> [...]
>
> Deelt de Commissie de mening dat de strafmaat voor inbreuken op de whereabouts en de beroepsprocedure op Europees en internationaal niveau beter gecoördineerd dient te worden?" (Belet, 2009b)

The tone of the Dutch original can be recognised in the English translation, too (Belet, 2009a). These frank questions led to an equally frank and clear statement from the Commission, albeit one emphasising the need for a balanced solution:

> "The Commission is fully committed to the fight against doping in sport and supports the development of efficient anti-doping measures in line with EU law provisions on fundamental rights and freedoms. The Commission is in regular contact with the relevant institutions and organisations, notably with the European Parliament, the Member States, the Council of Europe and the World Anti-Doping Agency (WADA) to discuss matters related to the fight against doping. The issue of data protection and protection of privacy of individual sportspeople is one of the most important and sensitive topics. In this context the Commission, following the opinion adopted in April 2009 by the "Article 29 Working Party" set up under Directive 95/46/EC on Personal Data Protection, has requested the World Anti-Doping Agency (WADA) to revise the relevant International Standard for the Protection of Privacy and Personal Information. [...]" (Belet, 2009a).

The Commission thereby referred the problem to established EU structures acting within the framework of enforceable EU secondary law: an example of "regulation", even if most of the material quoted earlier in this section rather qualifies for the label "inspiration". Similarly, when MEP's presented their wishes for a future data protection legal framework, in 2011, their priorities were clearly for a more unified set of rules with a higher level of protection for citizens and tighter enforcement (in conjunction with the high age of Directive 95/46/EC, a law dating from the infancy of the world wide web).

The envisaged changes were not driven by sports or anti doping, as such, but rather by embarrassing incidents of data law breach, identity theft, etc., yet the legislative proposal presented by the Commission, on 25 January 2012 (European Commission, 2012) must, by all standards, have been one of the bigger news stories for those involved in anti-doping in the EU. Again, it shows the EU as having entered the headlines of anti-doping, not because of having acted in the sense of "inspiration", but certainly by having proposed stepping up "regulation" at EU level.

The European Parliament, too, may initiate and publish studies. One such study was commissioned to throw more light on doping in professional sport (European Parliament, 2008). These examples show, again, how the EU can act politically without being able to adopt binding measures: only the question of what is meant by "action at EU level" is an actor-specific and case-sensitive one. But as the material drawn upon in section has shown, while parliamentary questions are not legislative in nature, but political ("inspiration"), they may certainly lead to legislative action being taken ("regulation").

2.2.3. The Court of Justice (case 4)

Case 4: ECJ case law: "Action at EU level" may also be taken, by individuals, organisations, enterprises or national authorities, by bringing cases before one of the courts of the EU: Since the entry into force of the Lisbon Treaty, these have been the General Court (previously the Court of First Instance), the Court of Justice and the Civil Service Tribunal. While the Civil Service Tribunal only deals with cases brought by officials and other servants of the EU, the General Court and the Court of Justice are open to all and offer plaintiffs, in this order, the possibility of judicial review in two instances.

While sports organisations are keen on creating and enforcing their own rules, they (as NGO's) are generally reticent to accept that athletes may submit these rules and decisions taken based upon them for judicial review with the ordinary courts; this is no different at EU level than it is at national level, so that ECJ case law on sport has taken some time to develop. Nevertheless, ever since the judgement in the case Walrave and Koch (C-36/74),[19] it has been recognised that sports-related issues may be settled by the ECJ to the extent that they are economic in nature. While Walrave had confirmed that discrimination based upon nationality could would not be

---

[19] Using the case number, judgements and other texts pertaining to a case can found via the on-line search form of the Court: http://curia.europa.eu/jcms/jcms/j_6/

accepted (contrary to established practices in the sporting world), the Bosman ruling (C-415/93) of 1995 truly marked a watershed, as it put athletes' right to free movement on a par with that of other workers (and provoked a reshuffle of the transfer system in professional football). What these and other sport-related rulings also did was to show the sporting world that the direct legal relationship between the Community (now the Union), on the one hand, and its citizens, businesses, organisations and territorial authorities on the other (something unheard of in intergovernmental cooperation, where rights are carried by the participating states) could be invoked, in principle, in favour of athletes' rights:

> "After Bosman, the sporting organisations were suddenly and definitively stripped of their aura of inviolability. Even if they remain the primary regulatory authority within their respective disciplines and undoubtedly still have a wide margin of discretion to organise their affairs, they can no longer simply ignore the reality of Community law." (Van den Bogaert, 2010, p. 493)

While complaints depend on finding a "hook" in enforceable EU law (a principle greatly limiting the scope for anti-doping related litigation inasmuch as the EU has not legislated specifically about anti-doping), it is nevertheless natural that some test cases should emerge to seek clarity as to whether this type of subject matter does or does not qualify for judicial review at EU level. It is in this light that the Meca Medina and Majcen case should be seen, which was adjudicated by the Court of First Instance in 2004 (T-313/02) and by the Court of Justice in 2006 (C-519/04). That the plaintiffs never achieved what they had aimed at, is less decisive than the fact that the CFI and ECJ recognised being competent to deal with anti-doping related issues, thereby rejecting the idea that such rules would be so "sport-specific" as to lie outside of their competence. When their positive tests had already been reviewed and their bans halved by the bodies of the sports sector, the two swimmers challenged the relevant anti-doping rules of the IOC and FINA (swimming) with reference to a scientific article indicating the possibility of endogeneous formation of the incriminating substance, nandrolone, via metabolism generated by consumption of uncastrated boar meat. The swimmers now turned to the Commission with a claim that their freedom of establishment under article 49 TEC had been violated, and that a collusion falling under the scope of articles 81-82 was at hand, but their complaint was rejected by the Commission, a decision which was challenged before the CFI and again (appealing against the CFI's judgement) before the ECJ.

> "In their complaint, the applicants challenged the compatibility of certain regulations adopted by the IOC and implemented by FINA and certain

practices relating to doping control with the Community rules on competition and freedom to provide services. First of all, the fixing of the limit at 2 ng/ml is a concerted practice between the IOC and the 27 laboratories accredited by it. [...] Also, the IOC's adoption of a mechanism of strict liability and the establishment of tribunals responsible for the settlement of sports disputes by arbitration (the CAS and the ICAS) which are insufficiently independent of the IOC strengthens the anti-competitive nature of that limit." (CFI, at 16)

The claimants never achieved the annulment of the Commission's decision they had demanded, but they sparked the development of a reasoning by the CFI and ECJ, which may be taken up in future litigation. The CFI had gone very far in terms of separating sporting and business activities completely in a way which must be welcome to all sports organisations:

"It must also be made clear that sport is essentially a gratuitous and not an economic act, even when the athlete performs it in the course of professional sport. In other words, the prohibition of doping and anti-doping rules concern exclusively, even when the sporting action is performed by a professional, a non-economic aspect of that sporting action, which constitutes its very essence." (CFI, at 45)

Yet the devil is in the detail, and the (widely quoted) English version of the judgement is a translation, whereas the (less well-known) French version is the original; the latter operates a fine distinction:

"Il faut par ailleurs souligner que le geste sportif est, dans son essence même, un acte gratuit, non économique, et cela alors même que l'athlète l'accomplit dans le cadre d'une activité sportive professionnelle." (CFI, at 45)

Clearly, "sport" (a sector as well as an individual and collective activity) is not the same as "le geste sportif" (a largely individual, concrete activity). While the CFI chose to disregard the economic consequences of doping sanctions, the ECJ chose not to:

"However, the penal nature of such anti-doping rules and the magnitude of the penalties applicable if they are breached are capable of producing adverse effects on competition because they could, if penalties were ultimately to prove unjustified, result in an athlete's unwarranted exclusion from sporting events, and thus in impairment of the conditions under which the activity at issue is engaged in. It follows that, in order not to be covered by the prohibition laid down in Article 81(1) EC, the restrictions thus imposed by those rules must be limited to what is necessary to ensure the proper conduct of competitive sport. Rules of that kind could indeed prove excessive by virtue of, first, the conditions laid down for establishing the dividing line between circumstances which amount to doping in respect of which penalties may be imposed and those which do not, and second, the severity of those penalties." (ECJ, summary, at 3)

Although this judgement was narrowly limited to EU competition law rules, and although the lawsuits did not produce the intended effects in the short term, the ECJ did thereby prove invaluable guidance to those involved in assessing the compatibility of anti-doping rules with statutory rules, such as those laid down in data protection laws. Its insistence upon the need to guarantee a certain degree of proportionality is known to have been widely observed in various fora: even if this is not a matter of "regulation" (as the ECJ cannot be said to have impacted directly upon anti-doping rules), there is clearly a case for "inspiration".

The CFI and ECJ rulings "are of the utmost importance in the sense that it was the first time that the Court directly applied competition law to the 'organisational' rules of sport" (Anderson, 2010, p. 347), thereby going a step further than the Bosman ruling did. According to one legal opinion, Meca Medina therefore

"has the credentials to become a new paradigm judgement" (Van den Boogaert, 2010, p. 494).

Against this backdrop, the case brought before the General Court, in 2010, by tennis professional Guillermo Ignacio Cañas (T-508/09) deserves some attention. The case is quite similar to Meca Medina, in that Cañas sought protection is his rights as a market participant, rather than as a citizen (it is interesting to note that, to this day, no lawsuit has been based upon EU data protection law), and because the Commission did not wish to take his complaint, which prompted the appellant to take the Commission to court. The Commission found the alleged competition law breaches to be exaggerated or construed (see European Commission, 2009a, at 51), but the applicant has sought annulment of the Commission's decision of the Commission. A true novelty could be observed when, by order of 25 October 2010, the President authorised WADA to intervene (see case T-508/09 on-line): in applying thus, WADA acknowledge the relevance of the EU courts, which may have a lasting symbolic and psychological effect in the world of sport, notwithstanding the recurrent statements to the effect that anti-doping rules are *sui generis* (WADA, 2009b, p. 18). But although Meca Medina has been felt, in some quarters, as untimely and inappropriate interferences (cf., Subiotto, 2010), the Court has not shown a willingness to interfere on a broad basis, and claimants will need to find substantial legal arguments in EU secondary law (Callery & McArdle, 2011).

2.2.4. The European Commission (cases 5-9)

Case 5: The European Commission acting as Guardian of the Treaties: We have seen that the swimmers Meca Medina and Majcen took the Commission to Court for having rejected their complaint (Case 4). This example allows building the bridge between the role of the Court, in adjucating cases based upon enforceable EU law, and the most visible of the Commission's various roles: that of "guardian of the Treaties" (Article 17 TEU). For while the Commission, as the executive branch of the EU, has a variety of different roles – some with real regulatory clout, others with only very limited means to regulate and others again devoid of any regulatory powers – it is this role which is the best known in the daily news.

It is in this role that the Commission chose *not* to intervene in the cases Meca Medina and Majcen, as well as Cañas (see Case 4); neither did the Commission chose a hard-law based approach in relation to the two parliamentary questions asked by Belet and Bozkurt respectively (see Case 3). But it was also in this capacity that the Commission *did* choose to get involved in relation to data protection when, in 2008-09, a new dInternational Standard for the Protection of Privacy and Personal Information (ISPPPI) (WADA, 2009a) became the subject of widespread concern, not only under ethical and practical aspects, but also in relation to the legality of some standards under EU and national data protection law (for a detailed discussion, see Waddington, 2010). Significantly, however, the Commission did not intervene via direct regulatory action (as the relevant EU law was a Directive rather than a Regulation (Directive 95/46/EC), it could have done so only via an infringement procedure against a Member State, if this Member State was demonstrably not applying the Directive), but rather by asking the Article 29 Working Party (composed of the heads of national data protection authorities, acting as a collegiate body) for two consecutive opinions (Article 29 Working Party, 2008, 2009). The following is the narration and analysis provided by a British sport sociologist:

> "We have already noted that WADA rejected a request from European governments to postpone the introduction of the whereabouts system and that, in their second opinion, the EU's Data Protection Working Party expressed regret that WADA had not fully taken into account its comments on the draft Code. WADA rejected all the criticisms of the EU Working Party in an almost contemptuous manner, dismissing their opinion as 'incorrect' and 'inaccurate', and accusing the Working Party of

making objections based on a 'flimsy pretext', of using 'petty examples', of having 'unrealistic expectations' and making 'unrealistic requests', and of lacking 'any grounding in reality'. WADA also, rather surprisingly, suggested that 'the aim of the [EU] opinion is less to offer a balanced and accurate assessment [...] and more to promote other agendas', though the nature of these alleged 'other agendas' was not clear [...]. Given the choice of words used by WADA, it // is perhaps surprising that it should also have accused the EU Working Party – whose report is written throughout in very considered and restrained language – as being 'overtly confrontational'!" (Waddington, 2010, pp. 262-263)

The purpose of mentioning these developments, as well as the comments made by Waddington, is not to propose one particular interpretation to the readers of this chapter, but rather to use it as a powerful illustration of the impact which action taken by the European Commission can occasionally have – even when initiatives are taken re-actively rather than pro- actively, yet nevertheless rooted in enforceable EU law and the Commission's role as guardian of the Treaties.

Finally, in January 2012, the Commission responded to a call from the European Parliament regarding better protection of individual rights of data subjects. In its opinion on the Commission's Communication "Developing the European Dimension in Sport" (European Commission, 2011a), the Committee on Civil Liberties, Justice and Home Affairs (LIBE) had stressed the need to respect the individual rights of athletes (European Parliament, 2011a, para. 5), in view of the report presented to the plenary session by the Committee on Culture and Education (CULT). In its report on priorities for a new data protection legal framework, finally, the LIBE Committee had called for taking the existing rules as the basis for future, more ambitious regulatory framework (European Parliament, 2011b, para. 1-10). The Commission reacted to these invitation as well as many others by submitting legislative proposals for a tougher and tighter set of future data protection rules, this time based on a Regulation (European Commission, 2012). (While a Directive needs transposition into national law via specific national legislative measures, a Regulation enters into force immediately and has the force of law on the entire territory of the EU without any further implementing measures.) This move was not motivated specifically by data protection concerns in anti-doping (although they will have played a role), yet anti-doping became once again covered under a more comprehensive measure: certainly an example of "regulation from Brussels".

Case 6: The European Commission: other types of involvement: The Commission's involvement has, however, never been limited to the narrow confines of enforceable EU law; indeed, the vast majority of initiatives would rather seem to fall within a broader category of cooperation and networking (Kornbeck, 2006, 2008; Szyszczak, et al., 2007; Tokarski, et al., 2004, pp. 71-78).

"Domestic" political cooperation within the EC/EU, essentially involving the Governments of Member States, was described in the examples where the Council was in the lead in the early and late 1990s as well as, after the entry into force of the Lisbon Treaty, the new initiatives of the Council in the field of sport (Case 1-2). The Commission has also presented its own analysis and proposals, including in two Communications (European Commission, 1999, 2011) and one White Paper (European Commission, 2007a, 2007b). The "Community Support Plan", exclusively devoted to the fight against doping, formed the basis for the allocation of budgetary credits which served, in 2000-01, for funding many anti-doping projects (cf., Iapetos Consulting, 2003). The White Paper on Sport, a more broad-based policy document, included a section on anti-doping issues: its recommendation to Member States to address trade in illicit doping substances similarly to trade in narcotics (European Commission, 2007a, p. 5), while being a political statement without any legally binding consequences, nevertheless helped spark debate in Member States and was sometimes even greeted by sports organisations (Aagaard, 2007).

Many anti-doping topics have been discussed with Member States in the informal EU Working Group Anti-Doping (2008-11) and the new EU Expert Group Anti-Doping (2011 onw.) set up by the Council in its Work Plan 2011-14 (Council of the European Union, 2011a) (data protection, criminalisation, civil aviation, social dialogue, EU funding opportunities, ...) (see "European Commission (Sport Unit) documentation" at the end of this chapter). While most of these initiatives have been limited to the exchange of knowledge and good practice, attempts have also been made, by the Council, to strengthen EU unity within WADA structures (Council of the European Union, 2000, 2010, 2011a), yet the Commission's role has, in this context, remained a limited one, essentially focussed on the application of EU law to anti-doping activities. The more political challenges continue to be addressed by Member States, although increasingly, Member States seem to wish an exchange of views and possibly even a coordination of national positions within an EU framework.

International political cooperation marked the Commission's involvement in setting up the World-Anti-Doping Agency (WADA), just like the Commission has, for over a decade, represented the EU as an observer in the Council of

Europe's anti-doping groups. The terms of these arrangements continue to be defined by Member States: while in 2000, EU representation in WADA included one Foundation Board set for the Council and one for the Commission (Council of the European Union, 2000), in 2011 it foresaw three Member State Sport Ministers only (Council of the European Union, 2011b). Occasionally, this politico-international dimension has reemerged in the activities of the Commission, including with the organisation of a major EU conference on anti-doping in Athens (May 2009) where the Commission presented its vision for the criminalisation of trade in doping substances (European Commission, 2009b). The high political visibility of this conference, which WADA attended, was increased when tripartite (Commission-Council of Europe-WADA) negotiations on data protection were concluded successfully in April-May 2009 and an "enhanced" data protection standard was adopted by WADA's Executive Committee shortly before the Athens conference (WADA, 2009a). This achievement was highlighted by the Commissioner in charge of Sport, Ján Figel', in a video message, in which the Commissioner also reminded that a big portion of the problems identified in by the Article 29 Working Party (2008, 2009) had not been solved and needed a solution, to be found through future tripartite dialogue (Figel', 2009). Again, it will be seen that the regulatory role of the EU was playing a role, even if only on the sidelines, when the matter was dealt with on an essentially *bone fide* basis, not using formal procedures but rather informal cooperation and network.

Yet a survey like this one would be incomplete without mentioning the importance of cooperation between the Commission and non-state actors, for indeed, it is a striking feature of the EU (and one that distinguishes it from international organisations like the EU) that it has a privileged access, not only to the subnational level of public authorities within its Member States, but indeed also to businesses and civil society organisations. What follows as a cogently logical consequence of the fact that EC/EU law was established as an independent legal order, creating direct legal links between the EC/EU, on the one hand, and the subnational level of public authorities, businesses, organisations and citizens on the other – the doctrine of direct effect as stated by the Court in Van Gend en Loos (C-26/62) – became an increasingly researched empirical reality with the unfolding of the structural funds in the 1990s, when it gave rise to the theory of multi-level governance (MLG), a phrase coined by Gary Marks (1993) around the time when the Maastricht Treaty entered into force.

EU-level social dialogue, involving industry and trade union representatives organised at EU level entering agreements under the auspices of the

Commission have a specific legal base in Articles 154-155 TFEU. While the social partners are under no obligation to enter into such agreements, whenever they do so freely, the agreements do nevertheless become binding upon them, with the Commission acting practically like a notary public. In the field of sport, this framework of particular importance given that professional athletes are not unionised as regularly as other workers, and that the level of unionisation has traditionally been very low among internationally employed athletes. The services provided by the Commission are therefore unique and should be seen in the light of the realities in the sector. The EEAA Collective Labo(u)r Agreement includes a section 14.7 stating that the use by athletes of "psychotropic or doping substances, even casually, is strictly forbidden" (EU Athletes, 2003). Unlike large parts of the established anti-doping system, the Commission has consistently taken the position that anti-doping matters may be part of collective bargaining, should social partners be prepared to include it into their talks and agreements.

This has important ramifications for athletes' rights, to the extent that their are employed and unionised. In this agreement, athletes' unions have freely accepted "use of doping substances or procedures" as a just cause for dismissal (EU Athletes, 2003, sec. 26.11), while they remain critical of some aspects of current WADA rules and practices ("whereabouts" in particular). All these examples show the usefulness of social dialogue at EU level, including in relation to anti-doping. Although some may still fear that trade union involvement leads to undermining the anti-doping system, this collective agreement actually places specific unilateral obligations on employees without anything directly offered in return. This shows that anti-doping is finding its way into collective bargaining agreements – already established practice in North America.

The Commission has lent moral and political support to the process, by inviting union representatives to various editions of the annual EU Sport Forum; by making it clear that the possibilities for social dialogue offered by the Treaty naturally apply to social dialogue in sport, too, including anti-doping issues (European Commission, 2011, p. 13); and by funding some social dialogue projects, including a study on the working conditions of professional basketball players (UBE, 2009). Interestingly, this material shows yet another variation over the theme of "regulation" versus "inspiration": the basis for EU-level social dialogue is a formal one, directly anchored in the Treaty, while the Commission's role is partly a formal and partly an informal one.

Case 7: EU funding: As yet another category of "action taken at EU level" can be seen the EU Budget and its execution; for the EU Budget is a major policy tool, which achieves objectives in their own right, thus acting as a supplement (and a corrective?) to the EU as a "regulatory state" (Robinson, 2007). It is not the work of one EU Institution alone, but rather a coproduction, with an initial proposal coming from the Commission; the Budget being granted by the joint Budgetary Authority composed of the Council and Parliament; but as a result of tripartite negotiations involving the Commission; with the execution being entrusted to the Commission under the auspices of the Council and Parliament; subject to judicial review by the Court; and subject to audit by the Court of Auditors. As such, it does not fit neatly into the actor-based break-down operated in Case 1-6, yet it represents dynamics which can only be imagined at EU level. Finally, while the Budget itself if hard law in the true sense of the term (the Budget being a law of the EU), as its effects cannot constrain but only benefit actors other than the EU Institutions, it amounts, empirically, to a pure case of "inspiration" from Brussels. In so doing, it enables the EU to show the sport sector new possibilities and directions, as alternatives to familiar ones, by offering the "seed money" needed to prove the feasibility and relevance of innovative forms of cooperation.

EU funding obviously played a role in connection with the anti-doping activities of the early 1990s (Case 1), as well as the anti-doping projects co-financed in 2000-2002 (Case 6) (see the external evaluation by Iapetos Consulting (2003)); some of these projects proved to be rather innovative, including the first cross-national study of doping behaviour in commercially managed fitness studios (Niedersächsisches Innenministerium, 2001). Other parts of the budget have proven their relevance, too, albeit on a more punctual basis, funding such activities as the standard-setting laboratory networks funded from the Framework Programme for Research and Technology, CAFDIS (Concerted Action in the Fight against Doping in Sport) and HARDOP (Harmonisation of Methods and Measurements in the Fight against doping) (see CAFDIS, undated; HARDOP, undated), or research funding for a fundamental research project in applied ethics, as part of a bigger project on current challenges in anti-doping (see Dikic, et al., 2011). Doping prevention projects cofinanced under the 2010 Preparatory Action (*Table 2.2*) reflect the priority, spelled out by Member States and confirmed by the Commission in its recent Communication on Sport, for future EU action on anti-doping ton concentrate on prevention targeting amateur and recreational athletes, including in fitness settings. The Commission has proposed to "support transnational anti-doping networks, including networks focusing on preventive measures targeting amateur sport, sport for all and fitness" (European Commission, 2011, p. 6),

... thereby showing an alternative direction as opposed to the traditional anti-doping system with its strong (in many countries exclusive) focus on elite athletes in competition-driven structures and settings. Prevention work has the potential to offer something different, including as it does not need to focus on sanctions but may indeed seek to communicate its messages to athletes without venturing into discourses based on guilt.

Under a call for proposals published in 2010, three network projects were selected to test three different cooperation types in the field of doping prevention: one network of national anti-doping organisations (with partners from other sectors), one network of youth sport organisations and one network of fitness studio operators (public, private, voluntary) headed by the EU-level umbrella organisation representing this sector (*Table 2.2*). Intermediary results from one of these projects are discussed further below, as an example of the sharing of knowledge and good practice that can be facilitated by the EU (section 2.3.2).

EU funding may be available within various parts of the budget and it is largely up to actors within the field of anti-doping to formulate project proposals demonstrating that their work may contribute to furthering the already agreed political objectives of the EU in the field represented by a specific funding source. The funding of social dialogue projects was discussed earlier (Case 6): in cases where neither Member States, nor the sport movement are supporting this type of activities, EU funding may become crucial.

Table 2.2. Doping prevention projects co-financed in 2011-12

Project name, beneficiary, reference	Concept/idea	Partners
EHFA (European Health & Fitness Association): "Fitness Against Doping" (FAD) EAC/22/2010/004[20]	Recognising that the fight against doping requires a coordinated transnational response, the project will establish a network of partners across Europe and with other international organisations, which have experience and knowledge in this field. The aim of this network will be to provide for the first time researched information on the extent of doping and current anti-doping policies affecting the fitness industry. Establishing the prevalence of doping in the European fitness industry will require some primary data collection through quantitative and qualitative research using a methodology directed by the Polish Institute of Sport Anti-Doping Research Centre. The results will provide the evidence base for future targeted interventions within the industry and will start a network of best practice to further the fight against doping. The international partners of the project will provide examples and evidence of effective anti-doping practices and policies used in sport that can be adapted for use by the fitness industry. These will combine to help educate and inform fitness operators, club owners, and national associations on effective practice. Policy will be developed on how to better educate our workforce in the area of anti-doping	Fitness Industry Association - FIA (UK); International Sport and Culture Association - ISCA (DK); Instytutu Sportu (PL); Anti-Doping Research Centre (DADR) (PL); Hungarian Coaching Association (HCA) (HU); Associação de Empresas de Ginásios e Academias de Portugal (AGAP) (PT); Bulgarian Association of Health and Fitness (BAHF) (BG); Danish Fitness and Health Organisation (DFHO) (DK); Arbeitgeberverband deutscher Fitness - und Gesundheits-Anlagen – (DSSV) (DE); Fit!vak (NL); Schweizerischer Fitness- und Gesundheitscenter Verband (SFGV) (Switzerland)

---

[20] http://ec.europa.eu/sport/documents/calls/oo4.pdf

	and of the threat to the health of those involved in taking doping substances.	
Deutsche Sportjugend im Deutschen Olympischen Sportbund e.V., EAC/22/2010/015 – "The European Anti-Doping Initiative: Creating a transnational network to develop and encourage anti-doping education in organized sports"[21]	• Peer-to-peer networks of Anti Doping Junior Ambassadors (ADJA) in the organizations' youth sectors (18-22 years old) will be created through the education at Youth Camps. • Development of a catalogue of best practices and a EU Model for preventive Anti-Doping Education, testing of the model in the particular structures of the partnering(European-, National- and Special-) sports Organizations. Scientifically backed multi-media training tools (in the languages of the partners) will be produced to help the work of the ADJA as well as to disseminate the information, also to external individuals and organizations. • Seminars and conferences on European and National levels will be organized to encourage cross-sectoral networking, communication and future, long-term cooperation between the partners.	Federation Internationale Catholique Education Physique et sportive (AT); Federazione Italiana Aerobica e Fitness-FIAF (IT); Olympic Committee of Slovenia (SI); French National Olympic Committee (FR); European Non-Governmental Sport Organisation Youth (DE); Zentrum für Dopingprävention der Pädagogischen Hochschule Heidelberg (DE); European University Sports Association (Switzerland); Österreichischer Leichtathletik-Verband (AT)
Anti-Doping Danmark: "Strategy for Stopping Steroids – How to fight doping in fitness centres, a European Project", EAC/22/2010/037[22]	In order to disseminate and strengthen "the Danish model" and the European effort on doping in fitness centres the project aims to collect relevant data on the subject and gather this knowledge in a final report on status and efforts made in the matter so far. After having collected the data from partners on the project,	Anti-Doping Authority the Netherlands (ADAN) (NL); Stockholm prevents alcohol and drug problems, Centre for Psychiatry Research (SE); Karolinska Institute/Stockholm County Council Health Care Provision – STAD (SE); Polish

---

[21] http://ec.europa.eu/sport/documents/calls/015.pdf
[22] http://ec.europa.eu/sport/documents/calls/037.pdf

a conference will be held in Denmark in 2012 with participation of European National Anti Doping Organizations (NADO's), scientists, politicians and other relevant organizations and authorities. In this way the project will support the main objective of the Preparatory Action in the field 'Fight against doping' by fulfilling the following specific project objectives: • gather data from the project partners on their current national status in the field doping in fitness centres including i.e. any surveys on the national extend of the problem, national legislation and challenges for future work • collect, document and valorise examples of implemented efforts on the matter • engage organizations and persons relevant to the work against doping in fitness centres throughout Europe in networking and sharing relevant knowledge and experiences on the matter with a view to qualifying existing and developing new initiatives • prepare a final report with background data, description and assessment of efforts implemented and experiences made	Commission Against Doping in Sport - PANDA (PL); Cyprus Anti-Doping Authority (CyADA) (CY)

2.2.5. What do the seven cases show us?

All seven cases represent "action taken at EU level", yet the actors are different, and so are the actions. This diversity represented in the five examples point to the most central question of tonight's lecture: whether and how "action taken at EU level" may make a difference in relation to the fight against doping. These examples all represent cases for EU-level action taken to protect or strengthen the individual rights of athletes, usually because enforceable EU secondary law obliges the EU (in particular the Commission in its role of "guardian of the Treaties") to take such action. This is one type of EU-level action, discussed in more detail below, and one which includes elements of "regulation" (section 2.3).

Yet in addition to this type of action, the EU may also make a more proactive, and possibly more original, contribution to anti-doping, namely by supporting transnational multi-actor networks in relation to prevention work targeting amateur and recreational athletes within amateur and fitness settings. This offers a different vision for EU-level action, and one with possibilities for "inspiration" but not for "regulation" (section 2.4).

Many hybrid types of action can be identified. For example, in Case 1, these examples all represent a systematic use of formal EC/EU structures and procedures, leading to formal adoption, albeit of non-binding texts: should they be seen as a diffusion of ideas and norms (as opposed to imposing them), a "political pedagogy of technical assistance", as the author of one study of EU governance projects in Russia has put it (Prozorov, 2004): i.e., as the use of a certain type of soft power, or rather as essentially non-binding and hence without direct effect at the level of front-line anti-doping work.

All these examples show a mixture of different approaches. Following the cluster approach which is familiar to social scientists, we shall try to group them and, hence, to make sense of them. All examples show the effect of EU Institutions, but if the concept "action at EU level" is taken literally, examples could also be found where other actors have taken such action: trade unions, athletes going to court, Member States urging for action. Such examples are, however, located outside of the scope of this chapter.

2.3. What the EU can do

2.3.1. Providing more fairness to competitive athletes

By identifying the fight against doping as being caught *"between Efficiency and Proportionality: a role for action taken at EU level?"* the title of the chapter points to a tension which is familiar and acceptable in open, democratic societies ruled by law but which, nevertheless, does not seem always to be so self-evident in the world of sport: that a fair system of investigation, prosecution and sanction must accept that not all who are guilty can be found guilty and sanctioned. The tension related to the choice between uncompromising, intransigent zeal, as opposed to a wilful balancing act between the objectives of the fight and the rights of the people concerned, drawing on the commonly agreed values and norms of the society in question. As a working hypothesis, it may be considered whether the biggest challenge today is not to uphold the credibility of the fight, but rather to ensure that it is halfway acceptable to the kind of societies that we otherwise think we are, or would like to be: decent, humane, democratic and governed by the rule of law.

Defending the rule of law (*Rechtsstaat, État de droit*) is a natural role for the EU as it is a cornerstone of our common European heritage and involves an amount of "normative self-discipline":

> "This idea of government limited by law, is a key part of all Western legal traditions [...], and in each case is a cornerstone of constitutionalism understood as a value-based discourse." (Walker, 2010, p. 338)

If this is the lead value, the standard might be defined as measures that are "necessary in a democratic society", a concept used in the European Convention on Human Rights (ECHR) (Articles 8-10) of the Council of Europe, another key actor on the governmental side in the fight against doping. Just like the Council of Europe, in the case of human rights, the EU is active in the protection of citizens' fundamental rights. As the examples from the work of the Court of Justice (Case 4) and the Commission (Cases 5-6) have shown, the EU may occasionally be called upon to enforce athletes' rights, even if this enforcement goes counter to the aims of the fight against doping. However, what may seem like a contradiction is not one in reality, for in the long run anti-doping will be strengthened by becoming more transparent, democratic and respectful of the people concerned, as pointed out by:

"[the] CEO of the Netherlands Anti-Doping Authority who, in the context of the problems associated with the WADA whereabouts system, observed that 'making anti-doping policies more democratic also makes them more effective' (Ram 2009)." (Waddington, 2010, p. 265)

Finally, the rules of anti-doping are defined by the stakeholders of WADA, including European Governments; this is the reason why the preparation of EU comments to the Code Review was decided by the Council (Case 1). The first major contribution which the EU can make seems, based on recent experience, to lie in providing more fairness to competitive athletes.

2.3.2. Promoting the sharing of information and good practice

The field of the fight against doping is marked by an unusually high diversity as regards national responses to the problem. Some jurisdictions have dedicated anti-doping laws (e.g., France, Flanders, Spain) while others have none (e.g., Germany, Netherlands, United Kingdom); the relationship between governmental and non-governmental actors is highly dissimilar; and finally, the concrete expectations upon governments, as expressed in the World Anti-Doping Code and confirmed by Member States by ratifying the UNESCO Convention, have been implemented as differently as can be imagined. The size of Registered Testing Pools (the groups of athletes targeted by their anti-doping system based upon the highest level of obligations, including as regards the availability for testing and obligation to communicate so-called "whereabouts" to enable them to be traced for testing purposes) varies greatly (*Table 2.1*).

These unusually big discrepancies put NADO's in double jeopardy: those intent on seeing the fight against doping being strengthened even further may see the German RTP as being far too small, while those more concerned with athletes' rights, conscious that measures taken must be proportionate, would think that the Flemish RTP is disproportionately big and therefore unacceptable from a civic rights perspective. Even without intervening directly, the EU can provide its Member States with support by collecting and sharing information helping to know the diversity of national arrangements better; this may also have repercussions on the worldwide stage and thereby strengthen the standing of the EU and its Member States, even if a formal EU role cannot be found within WADA structures, taking into account that the three EU seats in WADA's Foundation Board are explicitly defined as seats for the representations of EU Member States (even if this means joint representation), rather than EU representation in an orthodox sense (Council of the European Union, 2011b).

Yet this potential role of the EU is not necessarily limited to information about national legislation and the rules of sports organisations. The EU can also support prevention work targeting non-competitive athletes, as exemplified y the three network projects presented in *Table 2.2:*

- EAC/22/2010/004 – Fitness Against Doping (FAD) (EHFA)
- EAC/22/2010/015 – The European Anti-Doping Initiative: Creating a transnational network to develop and encourage anti-doping education in organized sports (DSJ)
- EAC/22/2010/037 – Strategy for Stopping Steroids – How to fight doping in fitness centres, a European project (ADD)

As can be seen from the names of the lead organisations and partners, the project titles and the descriptions of the work plans, all three network projects represent different types of partnerships and co-operations. This approach echoes the rationale used, and the experiences gained from the Health-Enhancing Physical Activity (HEPA) network projects co-financed under the 2009 Preparatory Action in the Field of Sport (see Chapter 6). In this way, experiences gathered in one policy field may be transferred to another – of course, without prejudice as to whether or not the already tested principles will work there, too.

Only limited data are currently available at a European level, although the network projects co-financed from the 2010 Preparatory Action in the Field of Sport are making a contribution to improving the knowledge base. For example, the interim report from the Fitness Against Doping project managed by the European Health and Fitness Association (EHFA) shows that 27.7% of fitness centre customers reported using a food supplement, while 2.52% of respondents replied that they use performance and image-enhancing substances (banned substances and recreational drugs). This percentage varied considerably between countries, ranging from approximately 2% in some countries to over 10% in others. The most popular substances identified by respondents were anabolic steroids, stimulants such as amphetamines and "other substances" such as diuretics. Male users of fitness centres were more likely to take banned substances and recreational drugs than women participants (EHFA, 2011, p. 23). It should be noted that the evidence indicates that there is a need for further studies as well as information and education work to be conducted in this field (ibid., p. 25). In such a field, the EU may make a useful contribution without any direct intervention, simply because the traditional anti-doping system has, in most Member States, not be geared to deal with the type of challenges.

2.3.2. Regulating and harmonising?

As discussed earlier, the "sport article" of the Treaty, Article 165 TFEU, explicitly rules out harmonisation and indeed any other legally binding measures to be adopted at EU level (see section 2.1.1). Whereas it is to be conceded that legal bases for "hard law" based initiatives may be found in parts of the existing EU secondary law – be it in the sense of protecting the rights of athletes (including but not limited to data protection), or indeed in terms of intensifying anti-doping activities under an EU leadership (Röthel, 2000; Vermeersch, 2006) – the basic assumption of this author is nevertheless that such action is not to be expected. The structure of this chapter reflects an overall assessment to the extent that it seems rather improbably that this type of "action at EU level" would take centre-stage in the EU's doping-related activities.

Nevertheless, one important possibility to make a direct contribution in sense advocated by WADA does exist, in that criminal law harmonisation has become a possibility with the entry into force of the Lisbon Treaty. Peers (2008) has shown how this allows, in principle, to build common EU penal law in certain, limited areas, and Kornbeck (2010) has concluded that these possibilities could be used to harmonise criminal law response to the trade in doping substances, a trend which has been observed for some years at national level (European Commission, 2009b). The trend towards criminalisation is a natural consequence of the intensifying and proliferating trade, which WADA estimates to represent bigger profits, at global level, than heroin trade, presumably because it presents a lower risk of criminal sanctions (and in some countries indeed none) (Barroso, 2011; BBC, 2011). The Commission has proposed to "examine the most appropriate way to reinforce measures against trade in doping substances by organised networks, including if possible through criminal law" (European Commission, 2011, p. 6); this proposal could be fulfilled by submitting a legislative proposal for a criminal law harmonisation directive, introducing a common offense of trade in illicit doping substances (but not necessarily minimum sanctions) across the EU.[23] This would amount to an unprecedented case of EU action harmonising the laws of Member States in this particular field, although it remains to be seen whether a legislative proposal will be made. In this context, it should be noted that members of the anti-doping community

---

[23] Note that the EU proposal is only concerned with trade in doping substances, not with doping as such, wheras some legal scholars in some countries have indeed taken the position that doping should be addressed as a specific case of fraud and punished accordingly (Bannenberg & Rössner, 2006).

regularly voice expectations of harmonisation because they are used, from the World Anti-Doping Code (WADA, 2009b), to a more relaxed concept of harmonisation, as opposed to the one operated in EU law; this may occasionally pose a problem (Kornbeck, 2010).

If harmonisation is understood in a less restrictive way – which in fact amounts to accepting a use of its which places the corresponding discourse outside of the framework of EU law (indeed not an ideal scenario for the EU Institutions) – it will be noted that the HARDOP project referred to above defined itself as a "harmonisation" project (HARDOP, undated), albeit one concerned with the "harmonisation" of technical norms rather than legal rules. More surprisingly, perhaps, is the use of the word "harmonisation" made by two respected legal scholars in the field, presenting a publication on national anti-doping rules as a contribution to their "harmonisation" (Vieweg & Siekmann, 2007), presumably in the sense of a calibration of legal knowledge, rather than a systematic and legally binding approximation of legally binding rules. In sum, if "harmonisation" is understood in these and similar ways, it conceivable that the EU may occasionally make a contribution in the direction of "harmonisation".

While an EU-led coordination of the operational activities of anti-doping should certainly not be expected – see the parliamentary question about an EU anti-doping agency (Mavrommatis, 2008) – it is nevertheless obvious that the EU may contribute to an increased European unity in this field, be it by strengthening the voice of EU Member States in WADA (Council of the European Union, 2011b) or by consolidating the uniform application of EU and national legislation which happens to be relevant to the fight against doping, as typified by the Commission's proposal to replace the current data protection directive by a regulation (European Commission, 2012). Indeed, the promotion and (if necessary) the enforcement of uniform application of the law is not a mere coincidence, a spin-off of other activities or an optional activity of the EU, as "sincere cooperation" is an obligation flowing from Article 4 TEU (Treaty on European Union). Just like federally organised states need to define the obligations between the federation and the federated entities (e.g., *Bundestreue* in Germany), so may loyalty towards the EU be seen as a specific norm in EU law (Hatje, 2001), a viewpoint which appeared, years ago already, to be supported by EU case-law (Joos & Scheurle, 1989). That Member States have committed themselves by accepting the World Anti-Doping Code, including by ratifying the UNESCO's International Convention against Doping in Sport, does not affect this basic principle, as Member States' obligations under EU law prevail in case of conflict. Conflict between international treaty obligations and EU law are nothing unusual (Klabbers, 2008) and needs to be deal with according to the usual rules. In this respect, neither the fight against doping, nor the sport sector in general can be said to be any different from other sectors of public life.

Overall, however, the EU cannot be expected to become a regulator of the fight against doping *per se*; at the most, its regulatory activities may occasionally play a role at the operational level of the anti-doping activities, including at the front-line level (e.g., data protection).

2.3.3. General conclusion

From the material presented in this chapter, it will have emerged as obvious that the EU's contributions to the fight against doping – whether they have already manifested themselves, or whether they have hitherto remained a theoretical possibility only – show a mixture of "regulation" and "inspiration" within the meaning of this book (Chapter 1).

An additional concluding remark would be that EU intervention has often been unexpected and not seldom resented within the anti-doping community and the wider sporting world; this pattern is familiar from other areas (the Court's Bosman ruling was certainly not well received in its time), yet the role of the EU may slowly gain more acceptance. There is no fundamental difference between the objections employed in relation to an influence of EU rules on anti-doping and similar objections in the field of free movement: in both cases, what is at stake is the so-called "specificity" of sport, where the autonomy of organisations has to be balanced against the rights and liberties of individuals. But the idea that not only sport is different and special, but indeed the fight of doping is exceptional and qualifies for exceptions from the ordinary rules of society may be untenable, simply because the so-called governance agenda is putting the sport movement under increasing pressure to accept more transparent and up-to-date forms of governance:

> „Die internationalen Sportdachverbände (IOC, Fifa, Uefa etc.) haben sich mithilfe der Einnahmen aus Vermarktung in den Massenmedien und Sponsoring von *Gentlemens Clubs* in quasi multinationale Unternehmen verwandelt. Allerdings ist vielfach die Gouvernanzstruktur hinter den ökonomischen und ethischen Anforderungen zurückgeblieben." (Pieth, 2012)

Significantly, this is not a quote from an interventionist lawmaker, an activist or a trade unionist: rather, these are the words of Mark Pieth, the designated chairman of FIFA's new governance body, designed to eradicate alleged corruption within FIFA, in a guest essay printed in Die Zeit on 1 January 2012. Of equal significance is the fact that FIFA and UEFA share a vision of athletes' rights that is closer to the one promoted by the EU (see Waddington, 2010): the European and worldwide sport movements are diverse, and this diversity should be increasingly reflected in the governance of anti-doping activities.

Chapter 3
Play, Not Therapy: the EU's role in promoting health-enhancing physical activity (HEPA) [24]

"I can't cry and run at the same time."

(Leedy, 2009)

3.1. Introduction

The quotation chosen as the motto of this chapter refers to the use of health-enhancing physical activity (HEPA) as a means to counteract depressions (Leedy, 2009). This may be a less well-known use of sport and physical activity, compared with the prevention and treatment of overweight, obesity and related conditions (in this connection, the use of HEPA is probably well-known even to the general public), yet the catchy little phrase illustrates well how sport and physical activity can go far beyond the narrow confines of sporting competitions, clubs and their traditional activities. This chapter will show how society can capitalise on this stunning potential and, in a European context, how the European Union may make a contribution towards a more diverse use of this potential: a clear case of "inspiration" rather than "regulation," given that the Union does not hold powers to regulate in this particular area.

This chapter aims to identify the major societal problems linked to overweight, obesity and physical inactivity, and the policy challenges within the sport and physical activity sectors flowing from these challenges. The article will show how action taken at EU level, by the Union, Member States, sport organisations and civil society more generally, may complement action taken by the actors more obviously and more traditionally involved in providing sport and physical activity to the population. The chapter aims to show why the current obesity crisis, or obesity epidemic, cannot be tackled merely by addressing it as a public health or a consumer protection issue, important as these aspects are, since the role of physical activity in burning energy must be taken into account.

> "Lack of physical activity reinforces the occurrence of overweight, obesity and a number of chronic conditions such as cardio-vascular diseases and diabetes, which reduce the quality of life, put individuals' lives at risk and

---

[24] The author would like to thank Professor Roland Naul (Essen, Germany) for comments provided on earlier versions of this text.

are a burden on health budgets and the economy." (European Commission, 2007a, p. 3)

The chapter will also demonstrate how these insights can translate into priorities for policy change, as the potential of sport organisations and civil society more generally to provide health-enhancing physical activity (HEPA) to the population is reassessed in the light of the activities of these organisations. In the case of sport organisations, this involves addressing the role played by competitive sporting activities within a broader (potential or realised) range of activities proposed to citizens. The chapter will focus on how the physiological and medical perspective has been challenged by critical social science perspectives, which themselves need to be counter-balanced with input from other academic disciplines and other professions, in particular those most immediately linked to sport and physical activity, so as to avoid a "therapeutic trap" and rather address the issues in a positive, stigma-free fashion. The chapter will show examples of how EU funding may act as a soft policy-making instrument within an environment where no regulatory approach can be adopted by the EU.

3.2. Introducing overweight, obesity and physical inactivity

3.2.1. From societal problems to policy challenges

In the European Union, like in North America and many other developed, wealthy regions of the world, physical activity has been in decline while overweight and obesity have risen. This is paralleled by a situation where professional sport has risen to new heights, together with related businesses accounting for sizeable portions of GDP in many EU Member States. Sport takes up a big space in the public domain, including wide press and media coverage, yet citizens are increasingly unfit and suffer more and more from medical histories typically triggered by physical inactivity. The role of physical activity in burning energy is addressed: although it is widely known, even in the general public, it is not always fully realised, which has serious consequences for how the obesity issue is addressed in practice.

The aim of this section is to show, very basically, which factors condition this type of scenario, and to suggest the most obvious policy challenges: at this stage, the question is not what steps need to be taken, but rather which challenges need being responded to. As the obesity crisis is now recognised as an epidemic (James, 2008) or a pandemic (BMJ Editorial, 2006), the section aims in particular to show why a population perspective needs to be embraced and which are the implications of embracing them, be it as a public health issue, as a consumer protection issue or as an issue for sport and physical activity policy-making. Against this backdrop, the chapter will be able to proceed by examining different potential contributions of the medical community and, alternatively, social science and social work (section 3.3); but it will also show that challenging the medical perspective will not do in itself. Therefore, the potential of the sport and physical activity sector, including sport science and physical education, will be identified in outline (section 3.4) and propositions will be made regarding the potential of the EU to make a contribution specifically in relation to sport and physical activity (section 3.5). To develop these arguments, however, the considerations presented in this section are paramount, as they point to the types of response that may or may not be chosen, respectively.

To begin with, it needs to be recognised that the problems addressed by the physiological and medical communities are real (Bay Nielsen, et al., 2006; BMJ Editorial, 2006; Bouchard, 2000; Brettschneider & Naul, 2005, 2007; CDC, 1996; European Commission, 2008; Kornbeck, 2009a; Lang & Rayner, 2005; Martin, 2010; Troiano & Haskell, 2010; WHO, 2006); dismissing them as media-driven sensationalism is not a serious option (Schmid & Bojack, 2008), just like blaming the medical profession for addressing the issue, with reference to the power of that profession and its perceived need to exercise power (Larsen & Brinkkjær, 2008; Teilmann Petersen, 2008) is not a fully credible strategy. This is not to advocate in favour of an uncritical reception of all contributions coming from the medical community – consider sales strategies deployed by some pharmaceutical companies aimed at selling drugs to people rather than encouraging them to exercise – yet it is a call for taking physiological and medical knowledge into account when developing strategies to work with people in real life situations. While the need for action may have become bigger than the need for yet more clinical research, the available knowledge nevertheless needs to be known and taken into account.

Overweight and obesity are defined as undesirable medical conditions involving an accumulation of body fat, traditionally expressed in numerical Body Mass Index (BMI) values. Despite its crude nature (the analysis can be complemented by additional data, including skin fold counts), this classic instrument was first developed by the Belgian mathematician and statistician, Lambert Adolphe Quetelet (1796-1874), based on a simple equation of weight (kg) divided by height (m) square. The resulting values are grouped as underweight (BMI <18.5), normal weight (BMI = 18.5-24.9), overweight (BMI = 25-29.9) and obese (BMI = 30+) respectively. The critical boundary between overweight and obesity is therefore a mere numerical difference between values above and below BMI = 25 (WHO, 2006).

Striving to break the curve and reverse the trend is a decent policy aim, in the first place because of the quality of life of individuals (European Commission, 2007a, p. 3). Yet benefits go much further, making the anti-obesity agenda more than a mere wellness crusade: it is actually good economics. Health economy arguments refer both to the impact which obesity has on national economies (savings can be made on public health budgets), and to the implications for individual enterprises (productivity, competitive edge). In relation to the latter (public health budget savings), the rationale may be relatively well-known. According to the British Chief Medical Officer Sir Liam Donaldson,

> "the health benefits of physical activity extend across the life course and relate to cardiovascular disease, diabetes, musculoskeletal health, cancer, mental health and wellbeing. Adults who are physically active have 20-30% reduced risk of premature death, and up to 50% reduced risk of developing the major chronic diseases. Indeed physical activity in the prevention of coronary heart disease has been described by Professor Jerry Morris as the 'Best buy in public health'." (Donaldson, 2009)

Conversely, failure to invest in HEPA is bad economics: it does not only mean letting citizens down and neglecting their welfare as well as neglecting an important socio-economic good. The British Department of Health emphasises that inactivity is a "cost to the nation," estimating "annual costs to the NHS as a result of physical inactivity" as ranging between £1-1.8bn, costs to the economy on account of sick leave at £5.5bn and costs generated by premature death of people of working age at £1bn p.a., adding up to an aggregated £8.3bn p.a. of "costs of lost productivity to the wider economy" (H.M. Government, 2009, p. 15).

> "These figures represent conservative estimates for the costs of inactivity based upon available published data and they exclude the cost implications of other diseases and health problems influenced by physical activity, such as osteoporosis and falls – which affect many older people." (H.M. Government, 2009, p. 15).

The Department of Health further emphasises the results generated by a study commissioned to the British Heart Foundation Health Promotion Research Group at Oxford University. Looking at individual Primary Care Trusts (regional public health care providers in the UK), "the results based upon 2006/07 demonstrate an average healthcare cost of physical inactivity for each PCT of £5 million per year" (H.M. Government, 2009, p. 16).

But HEPA is equally good for the productivity of individual businesses because it helps reduce absenteeism and makes workers more motivated and fit. In this way, it also benefits the economy at large due to increased productivity input. One study found that for each intervention of €475 per worker p.a., the investment made:

> "yielded an average savings of at least €999 [...] due to a reduction in productivity loss. The potential cumulative savings were an average of €1,661 [...] per worker over a 3-year follow-up period." (Hlobil, et al., 2009, p. 919).

As HEPA is not limited to competitive activities, it should be noted that active commuting practised by staff may also benefit employers. Research evidence published in the UK in 2007 "estimated that a 20% increase in cycling by 2015 would result in decreased mortality valued at £107m, with potential savings to the NHS of £52m from reduced illness, and a further £87m saved by employers through reducing absence" (Darnton, 2009). One review:

> "[...] concluded with a strong evidence for a relationship with long-term sick leave. From the studies included, obesity seemed to be a significant predictor of long-term sick leave. Therefore, and considering the public and economic impact of obesity, interventions aimed at the prevention of further weight gain or the treatment of overweight and obesity are considered as relevant, both from the individual and the employer perspective." (Duijvenbode, et al., 2009, p. 807)

Not only is it important to avoid limiting the obesity challenge to one of public health and consumer protection: if a HEPA perspective has been embraced, it is equally important to recognise that HEPA can be provided in a variety of settings, by a variety of actors. Not only the sport movement, but also other civil society organisations, public authorities, for-profit organisations, etc., have a potential to contribute. This is why cross-sectoral approaches are recommended in the WHO Istanbul Declaration (WHO, 2006a), the EU Physical Activity Guidelines (2008) and many other documents.

According to the WHO's "European Charter on counteracting obesity" (WHO, 2006a), governmental actors at all levels should be involved in efforts to counteract obesity: "Appropriate institutional mechanisms need to be in place to enable this collaboration." (ibid., sec. 2.4.1). While this may seem uncontroversial when coming from a governmental organisation specialised on public health, the reference to involvement of other public authorities than those in charge of public health is nevertheless significant: too often, this is not the case, even in rather affluent countries. Of equal importance is the WHO's exhortations to civil society whose member organisations – including "[e]mployers', consumers', parents', youth, sport and other associations and trade unions" – "can support the policy response" (ibid., sec. 2.4.1). The WHO takes the same view as regards the private (for-profit) sector, including "sports clubs, leisure and construction companies, advertisers, public transportation, active tourism, etc." (ibid., sec. 2.4.3). The same philosophy pervades the EU Physical Activity Guidelines (European Commission, 2008), a document which makes an equally strong case for cross-sectoral, joined-up work:

> "Many public authorities with significant budgets are involved in promoting physical activity. It is only possible to reach the set targets through inter-ministerial, inter-agency and inter-professional collaboration, including at all levels of government (national, regional, local), and in collaboration with the private and voluntary sectors." (European Commission, 2008, p. 9)

The EU Physical Activity Guidelines note that actors within the fields of Sport; Health; Education; Transport, environment, urban planning and public safety; Working environment; as well as Services for senior citizens can make a contribution, and invite them to take action in this sense (ibid., p. 9). The EU PA Guidelines define good policy practice via text, examples of good practice and 41 numbered guidelines. The aim is not to replace the relevant WHO targets but to define policies which make it a realistic choice for the population to try and attain them. As such, the EU PA Guidelines address Member States' public authorities (national, regional, local level) as well as sport organisations and civil society more generally.

3.2.2. What can (and should) the EU do?

The previous section has made it clear that overweight, obesity and the promotion of HEPA are important societal problems and represent substantial policy challenges; but the fact that policy challenges exist is not a sufficient pretext for involving the EU, in particular because the Union only holds competences inasmuch as they have been granted by Member States in a specific Treaty provision (*principle of conferral*). The EU is one among several actors at the international or (in this case supranational) level, public as well as private, who can contribute to the HEPA agenda (Naul & Holze, 2011), but what exactly does this mean in practice? This section will show that the EU is able to make a contribution to the promotion of HEPA and the prevention of overweight and obesity; yet the section will also make it clear that the exact scope of a possible EU role must be determined, on a case-by-case basis, taking into account the legal nature of the EU mandate, for each particular aspect of the problem, as well as the resources which the EU Institutions can mobilise in the process.

The EU may make a contribution – although Member States and sport organisations remain the "principal actors," as political scientists would say – yet responses will differ depending on whether they are based on the EU's public health, consumer protection, education or sport competence. The consumer protection mandate (Article 169 TFEU) allows, under certain circumstances, to pass binding legislation, including harmonisation "in the context of the completion of the internal market" (Article 114 TFEU). It also allows for non-binding political cooperation and incentives measures. The provisions on public health (Article 168 TFEU), education (Article 165), vocational training (Article 166) and sport (Article 165) allow for the very same measures only. The focus in this chapter will be on what contribution(s) the EU may make under Article 165 via political cooperation and funding.

It is submitted that Member States could do more in order to raise participation levels. *Figure 3.1* shows a graph extracted from the 2010 Eurobarometer (TNS Opinion and Social, 2010) on sport and physical activity (a survey with a strong focus on participation levels and barriers to participation). The original map includes differences in red shading (here rendered as varioys grey tones) where the darkest tones show countries with the lowest participation levels and, therefore, the most serious policy challenges. These findings may be intriguing for some Member States; however, while public budgets for sport do exist in these countries, with important income generated by taxation and/or lottery monopolies, these do not necessarily translate into sports and physical activity offers for every citizen. This raises the question of how to use non-binding political cooperation with Member States, as well as the so-called structured dialogue with sports organisations, to push for change.

Figure 3.1. Frequency of citizens' participation in sport and physical activity (self-reported)

Country	%		Country	%
EL	67%		MT	38%
BG	58%		CZ	37%
PT	55%		SK	35%
IT	55%		FR	34%
HU	53%		UK	32%
PL	49%		LU	32%
RO	49%		DE	31%
CY	46%		AT	29%
LV	44%		BE	28%
LT	44%		NL	28%
ES	42%		IE	26%
EE	41%		SI	22%
EU27	39%		DK	18%
			FI	7%
			SE	6%

Question: QF1. How often do you exercise or play sport?
Answers: Never

Map Legend:
- 50% - 100%
- 40% - 49%
- 20% - 39%
- 0% - 19%

Source: Eurobarometer 2010 (TNS Opinion & Social, 2010), p. 10

It is further submitted that sports organisations in many Member States could play a more active HEPA role by diversifying their activities, so as to embrace sport-for-all and HEPA while maintaining their traditional focus on competitive sports also, much in the way this has been pursued by the DSB (today DOSB) of Germany ever since they opened up in the 1960s. The development in absolute figures is already impressive (3.7 million members in 1954, 10.1 in 1970, 16.5 in 1979, 20 million in 1985), yet the true scale of the success becomes visible when counting members as a percentage of the total population (7.2% in 1954, 16.7% in 1970, 26.9% in 1979, 31% in 1985) (Schimank, 2005, p. 118). These figures show that the currently very high German figures are not merely the result of an unavoidably beneficial German mechanism whereby sports organisations autonomatically reach out to society. Rather, they show that the German sport movement has learnt, year by year and decade by decade, to diversify its offer to the population and thereby to reach out to more and more people; obviously, an umbrella organisation whose constituent parts (regional federations and local clubs) count almost a third of all citizens as members must be different from an organisation reaching out to less than 10%. It seems fair to assume that the DSB included more competition-driven athletes in 1954, proportionately to its total membership, than it did in 1985. The implication is encouraging for Member States with less abundant cash flows than those of Germany; for West Germany in 1954 was the country of Konrad Adenauer's economic miracle (*Wirtschaftwunder*) so that the impressive growth recorded here cannot be attributed to an increase in national or indivodual wealth. In other words, high participation levels are not merely the result of high levels of wealth.

Finally, it submitted that the outspoken diversity shown in the material collected and published by the Commission does not merely represent a hurdle to take, but indeed also an opprtunity to seize: for where differences between Member States are particulary big, the potential for mutual learning (in an area without a binding EU competence and, hence, without any possibility of introducing harmonising measures) is high. This becomes clear from *Table 3.2* which shows differences between Member States in relation to where citizens engage in sport and physical activity, again a reminder that there is not one recipe for high participation levels. *Table 3.4* shows differences in barriers to engaging in sport and physical activity, while *Table 3.5* combines Eurobarometer scores with different other data: the implications are similar. (For a more detailed discussion of all Figures and Tables, see section 3.5.1.)

Table 3.2. Where do Europeans engage in sport and HEPA?

QF3 Where do you engage in sport or physical activity? (MULTIPLE ANSWERS POSSIBLE)
(IF PRACTICE A SPORTS ACTIVITY OR A PHYSICAL ACTIVITY - Base = 87% of the total sample)

	In a parc, out in the nature	On the way between home and school/ work/ shops	In a fitness center	In a club	In a sports center	At work	At school/ university	Elsewhere (SPONT.)	DK
EU27	48%	31%	11%	11%	8%	8%	4%	11%	3%
BE	38%	29%	7%	15%	9%	8%	4%	12%	4%
BG	45%	27%	11%	3%	3%	19%	7%	34%	4%
CZ	58%	36%	13%	6%	7%	9%	6%	7%	3%
DK	64%	32%	20%	18%	8%	15%	5%	8%	2%
DE	60%	27%	12%	19%	5%	7%	5%	8%	3%
EE	67%	27%	5%	9%	8%	14%	7%	12%	2%
IE	43%	25%	16%	16%	8%	6%	4%	14%	4%
EL	27%	63%	13%	2%	5%	14%	3%	4%	0%
ES	53%	51%	11%	3%	9%	5%	3%	5%	0%
FR	52%	26%	2%	17%	6%	13%	3%	13%	4%
IT	40%	21%	17%	3%	15%	1%	4%	9%	2%
CY	39%	32%	22%	6%	5%	8%	8%	13%	0%
LV	51%	27%	4%	5%	5%	10%	10%	4%	13%
LT	35%	35%	3%	4%	4%	11%	9%	28%	4%
LU	51%	16%	8%	16%	8%	9%	6%	12%	4%
HU	36%	42%	2%	3%	4%	12%	6%	18%	3%
MT	28%	49%	7%	4%	5%	4%	4%	16%	3%
NL	40%	32%	19%	25%	10%	9%	5%	8%	1%
AT	64%	24%	13%	15%	6%	8%	5%	10%	1%
PL	43%	37%	3%	6%	5%	5%	6%	16%	3%
PT	39%	36%	12%	6%	5%	11%	5%	4%	1%
RO	29%	24%	4%	3%	3%	6%	6%	26%	17%
SI	83%	31%	5%	7%	9%	11%	7%	8%	1%
SK	45%	41%	15%	6%	4%	9%	7%	9%	4%
FI	76%	32%	19%	13%	13%	8%	4%	5%	0%
SE	51%	25%	19%	31%	7%	12%	7%	3%	8%	3%
UK	39%	28%	14%	10%	9%	9%	3%	16%	3%

Highest percentage per country / Highest percentage per item
Lowest percentage per country / Lowest percentage per item

Source: Eurobarometer 2010 (TNS Opinion & Social, 2010), p. 20

Figure 3.3 shows aggregated scores extracted from the 2010 Eurobarometer (TNS Opinion and Social, 2010), including the two highest levels of participation reported by citizens. While sensitivity to cultural differences warrant some scepticism (did respondents in different countries actually understand questions the same way?), the graph makes it more than obvious that there is more than one way to reach a high aggregated score. Denmark has a lower score in the top category than Ireland, yet reaches a higher total score. The same applies even more spectacularly to a comparison between the Netherlands and Belgium, or between Austria and Lithuania. While significantly more people in Belgium report engaging extremely often in sport or another form of physical activity, people in the Netherlands are far more likely to be just reasonably active. From a public health perspective, the Dutch situation seems to be preferable over the Belgian situation:

notwithstanding the benefits from having a portion of extremely sport-minded citizens, having a far bigger group of reasonable fit citizens seems even better. While the very high aggregated score for the Netherlands might actually include active commuting (*in casu,* cycling) a sport policy analyst would look to possible differences in how the sport movement is encouraged (or possibly not encouraged) to make the activities offered attractive to ordinary citizens with more modest sporting ambitions. In a nutshell, this would be a representative yardstick for a successful national sport policy, and would stand for both sound and responsible use of public funds.

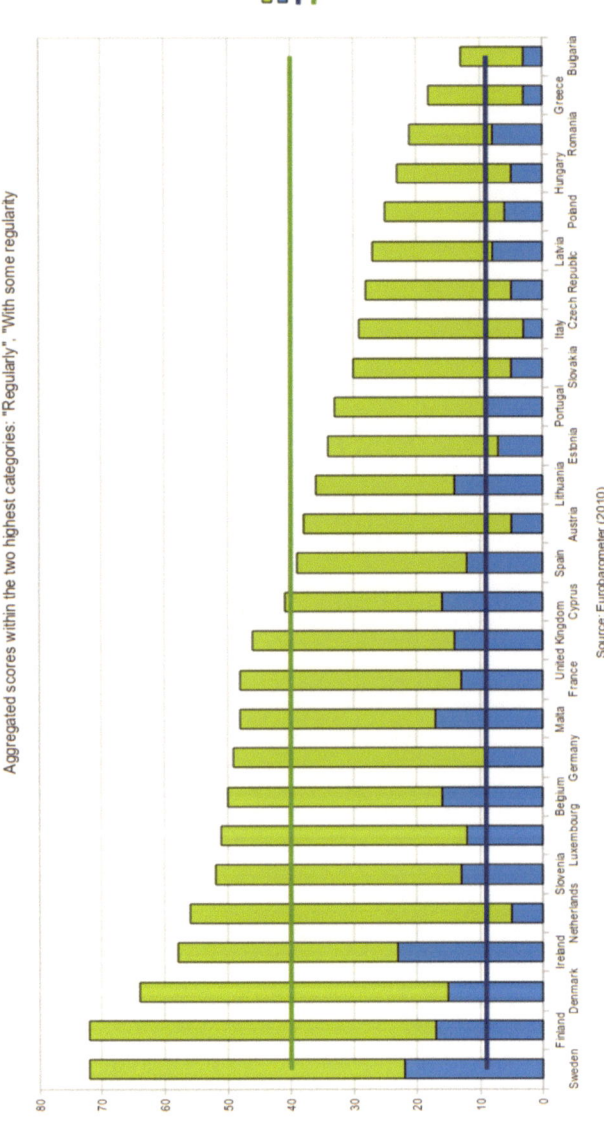

Figure 3-3

Physical activity frequency by Member State

Aggregated scores within the two highest categories: "Regularly", "With some regularity"

*Source: Eurobarometer 2010 (TNS Opinion & Social, 2010), p. 20
Design/concept: Jacob Kornbeck, drawn by Jens Griebel.*

Table 3.4. What prevents Europeans from engaging in sport and HEPA?

QF5 From the following reasons, what is currently preventing you the most from practicing sport more regularly?

	You do not have the time	A disability or illness prevents you from doing sport	You do not like competitive activities	It is too expensive	There are no suitable sports infrastructures close to where you live	You do not have friends to do sports with	Other (SPONT.)	DK
EU27	45%	13%	7%	5%	3%	3%	14%	10%
BE	43%	13%	10%	4%	2%	3%	16%	9%
BG	40%	13%	12%	5%	5%	3%	9%	13%
CZ	51%	17%	8%	5%	5%	3%	8%	3%
DK	45%	15%	5%	4%	1%	2%	18%	10%
DE	40%	14%	3%	3%	1%	5%	16%	18%
EE	37%	17%	5%	8%	5%	2%	12%	14%
IE	38%	6%	9%	6%	3%	1%	18%	19%
EL	51%	10%	8%	8%	4%	5%	9%	5%
ES	45%	13%	11%	4%	3%	1%	16%	7%
FR	43%	15%	6%	5%	2%	2%	16%	11%
IT	50%	3%	15%	6%	2%	5%	11%	8%
CY	62%	11%	2%	5%	2%	1%	11%	6%
LV	45%	13%	7%	7%	4%	4%	9%	11%
LT	40%	15%	5%	6%	4%	4%	21%	5%
LU	55%	11%	3%	3%	0%	3%	16%	9%
HU	43%	20%	12%	4%	5%	2%	9%	5%
MT	54%	11%	10%	1%	4%	2%	12%	6%
NL	54%	8%	7%	6%	1%	2%	18%	4%
AT	45%	11%	4%	6%	3%	5%	15%	11%
PL	46%	15%	3%	2%	8%	4%	10%	12%
PT	37%	10%	11%	13%	4%	3%	5%	17%
RO	57%	8%	6%	5%	5%	2%	12%	5%
SI	48%	11%	6%	6%	3%	1%	21%	4%
SK	46%	16%	7%	4%	8%	4%	10%	5%
FI	33%	16%	4%	2%	2%	3%	20%	20%
SE	47%	15%	6%	3%	2%	2%	15%	10%
UK	40%	22%	3%	8%	2%	1%	15%	9%

Highest percentage per country / Highest percentage per item
Lowest percentage per country / Lowest percentage per item

Source: Eurobarometer 2010 (TNS Opinion & Social, 2010), p. 37

Table 3.5. Cross-tabulation of Eurobarometer scores with other types of HEPA policy-relevant information

Member State	Eurobarometer score	EU Working Group Sport and Health membership	National physical activity guidelines preceding EU Guidelines
Sweden	72		
Finland	72	●	
Denmark	64		
Ireland	58		
Netherlands	56	●	
Slovenia	52	●	●
Luxembourg	51	●	●
Belgium	50	●	
Germany	49	●	●
Malta	48		
France	48	●	●
United Kingdom	46	●	●
Cyprus	41	●	
EU 27	**40**		
Spain:	39	●	
Austria	38	●	
Lithuania	36		
Estonia	34		
Portugal	33	●	
Slovakia	30		
Italy	29		
Czech Republic	28	●	
Latvia	27		
Poland	25	●	
Hungary	23		
Romania	21		
Greece	18	●	
Bulgaria	13		

Source: Impact Assessment (European Commission, 2011b, pp. 61-62)

The policy challenge, then, is how to promote such change, in sports organisations as well as in Member States, on an entirely voluntary basis. This points to the challenge of "opening up," the challenge of diversification within sports organisations and other civil society organisations which have the potential to offer sport and physical activity to the population: for the challenge of changing lifestyles is both situated at the individual and the collective level. It was already addressed by a major, EU-funded structured review, covering all the 25 Member States (at that time) and seeking to understand how children and young people's lifestyles had changed, and how this lifestyle change had led to growing overweight and obesity (as well as related associated health problems) (Brettschneider & Naul, 2005). This study focussed heavily on "sedentariness," and while this may be called a neologism in English, recent empirical research from Australia has indeed pleaded for adopting "the perspective that we propose is that too much sitting is distinct from too little exercise" (Owen, et al., 2010, p. 105).

> "It is our contention that sedentary behavior is not simply the absence of moderate- to vigorous-intensity physical activities, but rather, is a unique set of behaviors with unique environmental determinants and a range of potentially unique health consequences [...]. Our population health research perspective is on the distinct role of sedentary behavior, as it may influence obesity and other metabolic precursors of major chronic diseases (type 2 diabetes, cardiovascular disease, and breast and colon cancers)." (Owen, et al., 2010, p. 106)

Such realisations are important to make; inspiring, funding and disseminating them is a worthy clearing-house function for the EU. Yet it is even better if the action can be taken at EU level – by the Union, Member States and/or sport organisations and civil society more generally, in various combinations – to foster new types of cooperation whereby various actours with a proven potential to get people more active may start working together in new, hitherto unseen ways. Against this backdrop, there is a potentially important role for the EU as a source of inspiration and change: showing how these insights can translate into priorities for policy change, as the potential of sport organisations and civil society more generally to provide health-enhancing physical activity (HEPA) to the population is reassessed in the light of the activities of these organisations. Such change is contigent upon having the appropriate knowledge and concepts at hand: a challenge for academic and professional communities.

3.3. Challenges to academic disciplines and to the professions: physiological, medical, social science, social work, education and PE perspectives compared

But before the challenges regarding sports organisations, and the need for them to open up and diversify, are addressed, there is an equally big challenge found in connection with academic and professional traditions. For although the beginning of the argument has to do with knowledge generation, it cannot automatically be assumed that researchers, educators and professionals automatically have the best paradigms upon which to start new work; here, too, inspiration may be needed. Thus, this section will show on how the – more traditional – physiological and medical perspectives on obesity have been challenged by critical social science perspectives; yet it will also point out how these critical perspectives hemselves need to be counter-balanced with input from other academic disciplines and other professions, in particular those most immediately linked to sport and physical activity, so as to avoid a "therapeutic trap" and rather address the issues in a positive, stigma-free fashion.

3.3.1. Physiological and medical perspectives challenged by critical social science and social work perspectives

Overweight and obesity are on the rise and, as we have seen, this poses a serious challenge which policy makers need to add, but which are the exact root causes and what type of policy action should be envisaged? The choice of instruments depends largely upon how the challenge is understood and conceptualised.The causation of obesity via insufficient burning of energy needs ti be apprehended and appreciated before critical perspectives can be embraced. That the physiological and medical perspective should have been challenged here (too) by critical social scientists is not surprising. After all, the enormous prestige and power of the medical profession has made it easier for members of other disciplines and professions to portray medical perspectives as displaying some sort of tunnel vision. However, this critical perspective needs to be seen against the backdrop of the real and very threatening nature of the challenges posed to individual and collective health.

Overweight and obesity involve accumulation of body fat (WHO, 2006b), because the amount of energy consumed exceeds the amount of energy burnt by the body by means of body heat and muscular activity (Berkey et al., 2000; Jakicic, et al., 2001; Hansen, et al., 2007; Krustrup, et al., 2009; Wedderkopp, et al., 2001). However it is important to recognise that both factors (energy intake and physical activity) both have a bearing on the final outcome. Contrary to conventional wisdom, it is not obvious that Europeans' intake of energy (sugar and fat) is higher than in previous decades. One study of German children and young people under 15 years reported zero growth, while a Dutch study indicated that Dutch children and young people were consuming *less* energy than previously (Brettschneider & Naul, 2005, p. 59); in many cases, the daily intake is even reported to be *lower* than recommended quantities (ibid., p. 112). In the USA, consumption of fat increased during the years 1945-55 by almost 180%, only to drop during the period 1955-95 to a mere 60% of the 1955 figures. And while the 1970 level in sugar consumption represented 140% of the 1945 level, consumption decreased again to reach 100% again in 1995, thereby representing 90% of the 1945 level (Parisi, 2007, p. 104). At the same time, however, car and TV ownership rose on both sides of the "big pond" (ibid.), and so did overweight figures. Against this backdrop, it seems more than moderately justified to assume that the rise in overweight and obesity has been generated by a drop in daily physical activity that has been *more dramatic* than the reported decrease in energy intake. This would match the fact that there is no evidence that overweight children necessarily consume more calories than lean kids, while there is clear evidence that overweight children spend more time engaged in sedentary leisure activities, including TV viewing and video games, than lean kids do (Brettschneider & Naul, 2005, p. 112).

Overweight and obesity appear to be on the increase while physical activity is on the decrease (Brettschneider & Naul, 2005, p. 112): not just beause Europeans are not sufficiently often training in clubs and gyms (membership figures are actually historically high), but rather because physical activity has decreased spectaculsously in daily life. However, there is reason for hope as research has shown that physical activity can help bring a person's weight down and may improve their health status more generally, even if energy intake remains high (Hansen, et al., 2007). Physical activity may counteract a raft of chronic conditions which are often generated by overweight (hypertension, type II diabetes, cardio-vascular disease, etc.) (Booth, et al., 2002) yet somatic factors alone will not suffice to explain the occurence of overweight. Psychological factors are known also to be important (Wadden, et al., 1997). A study on hotel cleaners even pointed to a certain placebo effect: persons believing in the health-enhancing effect of their activity may produce evidence of an improved health status (Crum & Langer, 2007).

As a subset to the physiological perspective, the medical perspective may be identified. Both perspectives are indispensable and continue to exert a very great influence on political decision makers and the general public alike. The medical profession has a large interface with the public – which also gives rise to new training needs, not always covered via the normal medical school curriculum (European Commission, 2008, p. 22) – yet this perspective has become a frequent target of critique from social science and social work. While there is a need for the social professions to be knowledgeable about overweight and obesity – both because their causation can be partly social, because it tends to be more represented within lower socio-economic strata and finally because professionals may have to face the issues in their professional practice (Kornbeck, 2009a, 2009b, 2009c) – certain negative reactions to mere references to physiological and medical models (e.g., Schmid & Bojack, 2008; Walker, 2009) continue to form part of the reality within social science and social work literature. Drawing on a seminal text by Sobal (1995), and writing from a sociological perspective, Chang & Christakis (2002) state categorically that:

> "The medical profession and others have made powerful claims over the control of fatness, ranging from defining it as a disease to the application of a wide variety of medical treatments." (Chang & Christakis, 2002, p. 152)

While the role of the medical profession, in this connection, is obvious, statements like the one quoted may be misleading as they may suggest that the problem is more discursive than real. Nevertheless, there is no denying the discursive power held by certain sectors of society:

> "The causes, consequences, and management of human fatness continue to be a realm of considerable debate in both scientific and lay arenas (Kassirer and Angell 1998, Klein 1996, Taubes 1998, Wickelgren 1998, Austin 1999)." (Chang & Christakis, 2002, p. 165)

On the other hand, overtly critical and discourse-focussed debates may lead to flatly negating the objective facts of causation, including by promoting so-called "fat phobia" agendas, suggesting that individual and collective sentiments of urgency and desires to counteract obesity have a phobic dimension, rather than being rooted in a legitimate concern. That future dietetics professionals (students surveyed in a study) should display "a moderate amount of fat phobia" (Puhl, Wharton & Heuer, 2009, p. 438).

> "Obese individuals are also vulnerable to weight bias from health care providers. An accumulation of research has demonstrated that overweight and obese patients are prone to weight bias from physicians, medical students, nurses, psychologists, physical education instructors, and even health professionals who specialize in obesity [...]." (Puhl, Wharton & Heuer, 2009, p. 438)

On the other hand, if this bias influences the patient-professional relationship adversely, there may be a case for curriculum reform in the relevant professions, to "foster sensitive and empathic communication skills" (Puhl, Wharton & Heuer, 2009, p. 443). Nevertheless, whether it is legitimate for social scientists to promote a fat phobia agenda seems debatable. It seems to be all too acceptable for social science and social work authors to dstance themselves from physiological and medical models, including by making sometimes rather sweeping, unnuanced statements, such as:

> "In the biomedical and managerialist approach it is difficult to see beyond immediate, specific needs that can be provided in the current health and social care system." (Heinonen, et al. 2009, p. 150)

There is nothing to suggest that attitudes like this one cannot be found among many social workers who might be convinced of just how "holistic" their own practice is, yet they might easily dismiss physiological and medical contributions, thereby demonstrating the exact opposite of a holistic approach. But while it is correct, for instance, that it may be crucial to know that a person diagnosed with a somatic condition has suffered a war trauma (Heinonen, et al. 2009, p. 142-143), there is nothing to suggest that a medical practiotioner, departing from a medical perspective may not go for solutions encompassing non-medical types of – holistic – action.

Finally, the physiological and medical perspectives have generated vast amounts of knowledge which must at least be addressed. Although not all members of the medical profession follow new knowledge as much as they should, it is nevertheless striking that the first empirical study demonstrating that HEPA can prevent cardio-vascular disease was published in the 1950s (Morris, 1953), while the first study to make the equivalent link with cancer has been available since the 1970s (Polednak, 1976). (Both references are owed to: CDC, 1998; Martin, 2010).

While the physiological and medical perspectives are not sufficient in themselves to revert the trend, they are nevertheless indispensable. There is a need to develop professional *practices* (plural) within a diversity of fields, as well as practices of volunteers in certain cases, to work with people and build a behavioural change, rather than merely addressing clinical issues. This in turn may necessitate organisational change, if and when organisations holding the capacity to get the population involved in PA and sport are more interested in other activities; in particular if sport organisations are more interested in training for competitions than in providing HEPA. It is encouraging to see members of the medical profession publish about HEPA (e.g., Bay Nielsen, et al. 2006; Rütten & Abu-Omar, 2004; Sjöström, et al., 2006; Wedderkopp, et al., 2001), yet it is equally true that much research funding continues to go into clinical research rather than into action-related projects: this is certainly true as regards past EU funding, which has been considerable (see D'Amario & Froidmont-Görtz, 2005), and it may be assumed that national funding schemes are not fundamentally different in this respect.

3.3.2. Critical social science and social work perspectives and their limitations

Yet whereas social science and social work have been able to present credible criticisms of the physiological and medical perspectives, they too have their limitations; hence they need to be supplemented with knowledge and practice from education, physical education, sport, etc.: disciplines and professions less concerned with deficits. A "therapeutic temptation" or a "therapeutic trap" (Kornbeck, 2009b) may well be the biggest disadvantage of social science and social work based models of intervention. Whereas there is a need to get a debate started at all within the social work profession (Kornbeck, 2009c), it is equally true that any response is not automatically a good response. When one of the leading German social work journals printed it very first paper on obesity (Schmid & Bojack, 2008), the artice provided only two types of explanations: either lack of parenting skills in parents, or serious family problems, including emotional and sexual abuse. In any case, the authors called for counselling and psychotherapy as responses to the problems. Eating disorders and bulimia were covered, but not impossible working hours (not leaving time for PA), lack of access to active commuting, etc. These shortcomings were addressed in a paper published in the same journal (Kornbeck, 2009b), which emphasised the need to take PA needs into account in the first place: the widespread change at population level and the extremely high incidences concerned do not suggest that sexual abuse and bulimia should be the most frequent patterns of causality, while truly, physical inactivity is a cause for concern.

But therapeutical responses also come in various versions and have done so for decades already. Higham (2009), for instance, draws on the model of "transactional analysis" which has been around already since the early 1960s (Berne, 1964). It seek "seeks to understand how individuals communicate through their use of habitual patterns of relationships and behaviours, based on three ego states of the child, the parent, and the adult" (Higham, 2009, p. 27) and has been picked up by Kathy Leach, a psychotherapist, in a practical guide "for practitioners who work with people in situations where obesity is an acknowledged issue" (Leach, 2009):

> "Leach's aim is to help obese individuals develop adult-to-adult communications as a strategy for dealing with their weight problems. Her

> Transactional Analysis-based approach suggests different ways of thinking about and practising with obese individuals, with the goal of enabling the individual to make a positive guilt-free choice to tackle their obesity." (Higham, 2009, p. 27)

However, acceptance of this approach does not invalidate the claim that sport and physical activity must be considered as much as possible as a practical intervention tool: transactional analysis could well lead to agreement between the professional and the person concerned that HEPA is the right answer to the problem.

The social work profession and the public administrations within which many of its members practice (frequently on the basis of strong statutory powers vested in local authorities) need to be aware of the PA and HEPA option, so as to avoid overreacting. While it is true that strong obesity can be life-threatening, and while it is true that parents and guardians have a duty to promote the health and well-being of the children they are responsible for, it is equally true that the use of care orders to remove over-obese children from their homes is potentially damaging to these children's welfare. In late 2008, a six years old boy in the English county of Derbyshire was placed away from his home due to obesity and unhealthy lifestyle in his home. The care order had been appealed yet sustained (BBC, 2008). Also in late 2008, it became clear that at least six children in various English local authorities had been removed from their homes on similar grounds (Parry, 2008), yet what might otherwise have been interpreted as a typical Anglo-Saxon, risk-intolerant approach, was actually mirrored in a Mediterranean country: Spain. In 2007, a ten year old boy weighing 100 kg was living with his maternal grandparents following the death of his mother (from anorexia). Social services were tipped by the boy's school and had him removed temporarily. While social workers stressed that the grandparents were allowed to visit the boy, they were infuriated (Reuters, 2007).

Against this backdrop, a piece explaining why social workers should know something about obesity might seem perfectly innocent and uncontroversial: it was published in *Professional Social Work*, the membership magazine of BASW (*British Association of Social Workers*) (Kornbeck, 2009c). The article started by explainig the most basic physiological facts and the role of PA (as explained earlier in this chapter), and it was followed by another piece, with tips for social work practice (Higham, 2009). Yet my contribution triggered a rather indignated reaction from a leading British social work academic (Walker, 2009) who, while appreciating the initiative taken in principle, nevertheless pointed top what he thought to be "glaring omissions" and openly stated that references to medical models made my piece problematic. The response focussed on the need for interprofessional solutions (as had the piece it reacted to) and called for efforts to understand children and young people's physical and emotional well-being. But Walker went further than that, including by questioning the applicability of HEPA:

> "A depressed young person cannot exercise, an anxious child will eat to quell their fears. You don't have to be a Freudian to appreciate the oral and anal comfort gained from the digestive process." (Walker, 2009, s. 10)

The quotation stands out, not merely becase of its obvious and rather simplistic Freudianism, but also (and especially) through its unmitigated stance against HEPA. A professor and Head of Child & Adolescent Mental Health, Walker has taken the bold step to discredit a widely recorded practice of using HEPA to counteract depressions. Not only the medical community is aware that this approach may be effective (e.g., Bots, et al., 2008); comparable knowledge is avaiable even within the mental health branch of social work literature, including an article on running in depressive women (Leedy, 2009) as well as numerous entries and abstracts in the leading UK social work database, Social Care Online.[25] The example shows the need to take available knowledge into account before making an assessment of the instruments available to tackle a problem. And as can be seen from the last two examples, social work does have somethikng to offer, including specific counselling methods such as *transactional analysis* (Higham, 2009). Each academic discipline and each discipline needs to develop its own overweight discourse, while drawing on the knowledge and practice models both from the discipline or discipline themselves, and on those offered by others as well.

3.3.3. Sport and physical activity as a supplement and an alternative?

As an alternative to psychotherapy, there is good reason to look for solutions based on PA and HEPA, rooted in the traditions of education/pedagogy, Bildung and physical education, including the playful ("ludic") aspect of Huizinga's *homo ludens*. If fun and joy can be encountered, this will only make the interventions proposed the more successful. While this may be seen as a placebo effect, it remains that the recreational value – the fun effect – of a physical activity plays a health-promoting role. Entitled "Recreational soccer is an effective health-promoting activity for untrained men," a recent study from Denmark emphasised this recreational role of

---

[25] http://www.scie-socialcareonline.org.uk

soccer, pointing to better improvements in individual health status that could be achieved by running, although soccer players run less during the same time. While intensity seems to play a role, the recreational and social aspects of the game are equally believed to be instrumental (Krustrup, et al., 2009).

The English and Spanish care order cases, and the German argument for using psychotherapy, should be addressed under the perspective of proportionality: do they employ means proportionate to the ends they intend to further? Can protection from over-eating be rated on a par with protection from a sexually abusing family member? Could not a local authority chose, alternatively, to act on the basis of statutory powers and propose PA on a more voluntary basis? Could interventions aimed at individuals and their families be coupled with community-based interventions, thereby avoiding stigmatising individuals? Could local authorities reach out to local sports clubs and other civil society organisations, at least as part of the solution? All these considerations naturally lead to considering the potential and actual roles of sports organisations and civil society more generally. For if we accept sport and physical activity as a supplement and an alternative, possibly also as a corrective to the medical and socio-therapeutic approaches, we must address the question what should be done to use sport and physical activity on a large scale as a tool fomenting change and counteracting obesity.

3.4. What role for the sport and physical activity sector?

From the remarks made above about the need for all sectors to contribute to obesity prevention and treatment; on the shortcomings of an exclusively medical approach; as well as from the critical stance taken with regard to simplistically critical social science and social work discourses and responses, it will be evident that there is need for education, sport science and the sport movement to make a contribution: not only within their own remits, but also – and particularly – in partnership with other sectors and professions. This presents and sport sector with a number of challenges of an organisational and cultural nature.

> "As a tool for health-enhancing physical activity, the sport movement has a greater influence than any other social movement. Sport is attractive to people and has a positive image. However, the recognised potential of the sport movement to foster health-enhancing physical activity often remains under-utilised and needs to be developed." (European Commission, 2007a, pp. 3-4)

The first challenge has to do with the intrinsic value of sport and physical activity. The dilemma relates to the simultaneous need to preserve the attraction of a sector organised around essentially non-utilitarian values, and to ensure that a crucial (if not the most crucial) contributor is not missing in the overall anti-obesity effort. A commonplace English joke has it that explaining a joke is like dissecting a frog: no-one is amused the frog dies. Indeed, the same may be said with respect to making the sport sector of tool for the promotion of any extrinsic value and agenda, yet the attempt ought to be made.

Within the sport and physical activity community, there is an understandable fear of instrumentalisation. The vitality and enormous outreach of this biggest social movement in Europe reflects its immediate attractiveness and attraction. The challenge is, how can we mobilise a movement than draws its strength from its bottom-up dynamics without ruining its vitality in a top-down fashion? By borrowing from Nietzsche, it is the Dyonesian (pleasure-driven) rather than the Apollonic (rational) principle that is its strength. The fact that so many Copenhageners keep healthy by cycling (Copenhagen is often showcased internationally for this), reflects the fact that they take pleasure in cycling. The same applies to volunteering where the marked differences between Member States correspond with differences in the population's perception of volunteering. One study commissioned by the Commission The report found:

> "significant differences between Member States with regard to the proportion of volunteers in relation to Member States' adult population for the same year. It appears that volunteering in sport represents a significant share of the adult population in Finland (16%), Ireland (15%), the Netherlands (12-14%), Denmark (11%), Germany (10.9%) and Malta (9.2%). Conversely, in Estonia (1.1%), Greece (0.5%), Lithuania (0.1%), Latvia and Romania (less than 0.1%) volunteering in sport does not appear to be a common practice. These differences can partly be explained by the different traditions of volunteering in the sport sector. In countries where authoritarian or communist rule have given a negative meaning to the practice of volunteering, the number of volunteers remains particularly low (e.g. Romania); whereas in countries where the tradition of volunteering in sport is particularly strong, the share is much higher."
> (GHK, 2010, p. 176)

The same report found that in "some Member States sport is very high on the political agenda, something which is in most cases correlated to the existence of a sport/health policy. [...] However, the vast majority of Member States does not have a separate national strategy or framework for volunteering in sport" (GHK, 2010, p. 195). In each case, when it works –

active commuting or volunteering – it is due to the activity's inherent, intrinsic value as subjectively perceived by the persons concerned. This must be borne in mind by all policy developers, planners and decision makers because it sets these activities off from such activities as are directly motivated by an extrinsic reward. It was thus encouraging when a Danish clinical study showed greater improvements in health, untrained, 20-43-year-old males enjoying recreational soccer, as compared with similar Danish males practising running.[26] They obtained good results from an activity they perceived as fun (for although jogging is also enjoyed by some, the playful, social world of team sports may appeal more directly to more people) and the Dyonesian aspect appears to take centre stage.

> "Soccer training is highly motivating and appeals to a significant part of the population and therefore has the potential to be implemented as a permanent health-promoting activity." (Krustrup, et al., 2009, p. 825)

The fun of soccer among buddies appears to have driven these men to do a little bit more:

> "The two groups had the same average heart rate during the training, but with a much greater distribution of the heart rate in the soccer group, reflecting the marked and frequent changing in exercise intensity when playing soccer." (Krustrup, et al., 2009, p. 830)

From a methodological perspective there may be very valid reasons not to overstretch generalisations made on the basis of one such study. Deductions made from the findings of trials or surveys made in contexts determined by many specific factors may mean they come close to the "n=1" case. Giving that sport and leisure behaviour are shaped by culture, climate and other local factors – the Eurobarometer 2010 shows greater differences between Member States than many comparable Eurobarometer surveys – generalising on the basis of this Danish case might bear some of the same risks as quoting simple statements from Kinsey & Kinsey's study of American women's sexuality in the 1950s to make statements about women's sexuality in general. The example is not constructed but real and was taken from a chapter in a textbook published by a leading academic publisher (Mostyn, 2006). This is quite a considerable courage to display, given that the sample is so narrowly defined by cultural, ethnic, geographic and especially historical parameters. Nevertheless, if believe that this type of social change

---

[26] "36 healthy untrained Danish men aged 20–43 years were randomised into a soccer group (SO; n=13), a running group (RU; n=12) and a control group (CO; n=11)." ((Krustrup, et al., 2009, p. 825)

is desirable for a variety of other reasons, such a case is encouraging, less in a causal sense than because of its illustrative value. Instead of the "what works" question of evidence-based practice, it may be a case for an "it is possible" statement.

3.5. From analysis to action: taking stock of the potential role of the EU

Given that Article 165 TFEU allows for non-binding political cooperation and for "incentive measures" (funding), this section aims to identify the implications regarding possibilities to contribute to obesity prevention via HEPA promotion. It has been suggested that the Member States of the WHO Europe Region should undertake national reviews of HEPA-related policies in a coordinated way; and that:

> "These implementation guidelines should take into account the ethnic and cultural diversity in each European country. Involving relevant stakeholders such as policy makers, health professionals, other sectors and civic organisations would help maximise adoption, implementation and dissemination of the recommendations" (Oja, et al., 2010).

The same can be done within the EU, possibly in conjunction with the WHO.

3.5.1. Possibilities for political cooperation

The EU has a clearing house function, collecting uniform data on issues of common interest to the Union and its Member States and presenting them, chiefly in the shape of Eurobarometer surveys. The Eurobarometer is a particularly trusted instrument as it is based on face-to-face interviews rather than unsolicited telephone calls or web-based surveys. Created in 1973, they are also potentially a strong communication tool for the EU to use (Bogni, 2010). Sport and HEPA related Eurobarometer surveys have indeed led to quite an amount of PE and HEPA scholarship (e.g., Sjöström, et al., 2006; Scheerder & Van Tuyckom, 2007). In connection with the European Year of Education through Sport (EYES) 2004, a Special Eurobarometer was conducted in two parts, one immediately before the Year, the other towards its end (European Opinion Research Group EEIG, 2003a, 2003b; TNS Opinion & Social, 2004). In 2003, a survey was focussed on physical activity (whereas the two EYES surveys had been more narrowly focussed on sport) (European Opinion Research Group EEIG, 2003b). In 2010 the first combined sport and physical activity survey was published (TNS Opinion & Social, 2010). Already the 2003 Eurobarometer formed the basis for a seminal academic paper on HEPA participation (Rütten, A. & Abu-Omar, 2004). It is equally gratifying to see that one paper dealing with the problematic economic legacy of the Athens Olympic Summer Games 2004 both draw explicitly on data from the Eurobarometer 2003-04 (Tzormpatzakis & Sleap, 2007; cit. Pappous, 2011, p. 84). This shows how information collected free of bias by EU Institutions may be fed into highly political debates, at national level, regarding which investments to use public money for, in particular as regards the outcome for the general population in terms of access to sport and physical activity:

> "Hosting the Games is a notoriously expensive operation and the IOC and national governments have to justify the huge cost and investments. The 2004 Athens Olympic Games had an overall cost of $11 billion, almost double the initial budget. Six years later, Greece has just requested a €45bn bailout package from the EU and International Monetary Fund to avoid bankruptcy. Currently criticism has sharpened and voices are raised arguing that the 2004 Olympic spending played an important part in helping Greece fall into debt crisis (Gatopoulos, 2010). Concerns centre around the huge investments governments put into sport and organisers of the forthcoming 2012 Olympics in London have recently announced that $39 million is to be cut from the London Olympic budget (Associated Press, 2010)." (Pappous, 2011, p. 81)

Arguably, the most recent Eurobarometer (TNS Opinion & Social, 2010) is also the most innovative and the one which points most directly to political hotspots, some of which have been extracted for illustration in this chapter. First, the frequency of citizens' participation in sport and physical activity (self-reported figures) is markedly varied, as the map show different shadings of red, ranging from very dark to very light (*Figure 6.1*). As noted in the EU Physical Activity Guidelines (European Commission, 2008, p. 9), and as discussed above, this is not merely a split between affluent and less-affluent Member States, given that public sport budgets exist in all Member States, and that state-of-the art facilities have been built, in recent years, to host such competitions as the football Euro (Portugal) and the Summer Olympics (Greece). Yet the figures entice the observer to ask for background information, and invite him or her to cross-tabulate them with other types of information about the same countries, precisely because differences are so unsually big:

> "The survey's results show large, sometimes even very large, disparities among Member States on many questions. Some of them show a high level of participation in sport and physical activities and seem to be a step ahead in the provision of sporting and physical activity opportunities to their citizens. This indicates that sport and physical activity are an area where big gains can be made by identifying and spreading good practices

between different Member States and different organisations." (TNS Opinion & Social, 2010, p. 63)

If we ask where Europeans engage in sport and HEPA (*Table 6.2*), again a heterogeneous pattern presents itself, and one which shows that sport and PA are offered under very different arrangements in Member States; this has implications for what makes a good policy in favour participation. In this connection it should be remembered, in particular, that physical activity is far broader than sport (whether organised or not, competitive or not) and that it includes such practices as, for instance, active commuting (walking, cycling).

As discussed above, sports volunteering is organised very differently across the EU (GHK, 2010), and the same pattern appears to apply to the sport sector more generally. One of the implications of this diversity is that uniform HEPA policy recommendations, following a "one size fits all" logic, make little sense, as the feasibility of policy choices regarding people's access to sport and physical activity is greatly influenced by the national context. But before looking at differences located at the policy level, it is still rewarding to study differences in the actual sport and physical activity of the populations. The Eurobarometer 2010 (TNS Opinion & Social, 2010, p. 10) includes figures on people's self-reported frequency of sport and physical activity practice. Not only are the rough figures (*Figure 3.1*) noteworthy for producing a league table rather similar to league tables on socio-economic matters (including regarding the current crisis); they are even more significant if the highest and the second-highest scores are compounded.

> "While cultural, climatic and financial differences may be expected to influence these scores, it will be noticed that the picture is not one of a clear-cut north/south or east/west split. For example, Finland/Estonia, Cyprus/Greece and Spain/Portugal are pairs of countries displaying larger disparities than might have been expected." (European Commission (2011b, p. 60)

The result shows not merely how many very sports-minded people a country has, but indeed how many people are reasonably active (*Table 3.3*), and this exercise produces a more nuanced picture of the EU. While critics may argue that these scores are likely to reflect some bias – including cultural differences and variegating perceptions of sport and physical activity (which may mean that people understand the questions differently) – it is nevertheless very interesting to compare and contrast, for instance, the aggregated scores of Belgium and the Netherlands, as discussed above (see 6.2.2). They show a different mixture of very intensive and reasonable physical activity behaviour: whatever the exact root causes, a successful sport policy and a successful HEPA policy is not necessarily one leading to many people being very frequently training *or* biking, but rather one enabling most people to maintain a level of activity that is inductive to good health.

> "The more physically active countries are overall clustered in the Northern part of the EU, while the less active are mainly the Southern countries and the new Member States. This is most probably a sign that the organisation of society, particularly in the planning of working and leisure time as well as for economic reasons, plays a key role in the area of citizens' participation in sport and physical activities. It may also reflect differences in the organisation of physical activity and sport in Member States, including financing issues and spending priorities in the field of sport." (TNS Opinion & Social, 2010, p. 63)

This type of cross-tabulation illustrates how an EU-level clearinghouse function may benefit national policy development – "inspiration from Brussels". It has been tested in the academic community, including a study of PA participation levels in Greece and the consequences of the heavy investments made in the Athens Summer Games 2004 (Tzormpatzakis & Sleap, (2007), and it has been practised by the Commission in a policy document, in this case including additional categories of information (*Table 3.5*). It should lead to a re-examination of the evidence available on barriers to participation, including evidence generated by the Eurobarometer 2010, for although barriers are partly specific to individuals, they are also partly (and largely) reflections of structures and thus shared by people at the population level. Again, the differences between Member States are considerable (*Table 3.4*); yet this should not merely be seen as a handicap or an impediment to cooperation: rather, it may also be interpreted as a justification for mutual learning, in particular within EU-funded networks. That such networks can be of different types, is obvious to the Commission, which is why the nine HEPA projects which were selected for funding during the year 2010 all represent different types of partnerships, participating organizations, activities and concepts (*Table 3.6*). This has profound policy implications, as noted by the contractor having conducted the Eurobarometer 2010 survey:

> "The survey's results therefore suggest that policy makers at all levels should take into account the impact that different policies have on citizens' opportunities to play sports or be physically active, and steer those policies towards a more sport and physical activity-friendly approach." (TNS Opinion & Social, 2010, p. 63)

Whether all Member States' Governments will wish to compare and coordinate their policies into a more HEPA-friendly direction, is a political question the outcome of which remains to be seen. But while a cursory examination of the evidence might suggest a simple north-south split (a least on general, cross-cutting issues), the reality is more complex. The United Kingdom is not only a country with high obesity levels, more like a Mediterranean than like a Northern European country, it is also a country whose national sports policies have been redirected very strongly towards rewarding organisations for having won Olympic medals at the last Games: as noted by a late British academic, "[a]ny resistance to the drive for Olympic medals is somewhat fragile" (Green, 2006, p. 227). Indeed,

> "[...] such is the currency of the narrative storyline around elite achievement at the highest political and institutional levels in the UK, that 'alternative voices' arguing for some perspective in respect of spending such large amounts of public money on the aspirational goal of a handful of Olympic medals, remain relatively suppressed." (Green, 2006, p. 233)

Yet there are differences which may make it reasonable to be more optimistic this time, and these differences relate to deliberate policy choices, with Spain's planning of the Barcelona Summer Games 1992 still standing out as an example for emulation. The London Summer Games 2012 still stand out for having a strategy for raising participation levels (Weed, et al., 2008), and may thus succeed. While hosting the 2004 Games appears to have been a fatal investment error by Greece, the evidence indicates that there may be a reverse correlation between the level of sport policy, participation and HEPA policy development of a country, on the one hand, and the risks it runs by hosting major international events on the other:

> "For developed economies with existing infrastructure, stadiums, and large-scale event management experience, prudently managed events can potentially produce a net profit. For developing economies that need new facilities, however, these events are a risky and irrational development plan. To developing economies with host-country dreams: forego the Olympic and World Cup glory and spend your taxpayers' dollars on projects that will actually benefit them for the long term." (Bray, 2011, p. 101)

Thus, evidence is available which may inform a political process at EU level, should there by a willingness to run a monitoring mechanism, preferably based on the EU Physical Activity Guidelines, to compared Member States HEPA-related policies. Proposals to this effect are laid out in the Commission's 2011 Communication on Sport:

"Commission and Member States: based on the EU Physical Activity Guidelines, continue progress toward the establishment of national guidelines, including a review and coordination process, and consider proposing a Council Recommendation in this field.

Commission: support transnational projects and networks in the area of health-enhancing physical activity." European Commission (2011a, p. 7)

The rationale behind these proposals, including the cross-tabulation exercise described above, is presented in Annex III to the Impact Assessment (European Commission (2011b, pp. 59-62). A similar, non-binding mechanism exists in the field of Health, based on the EU Strategy (Council of the European Union, 2008); whether such a mechanism will become reality in the field of Sport, depends on political processes, including the wake of the 2011 EU Work Plan on Sport (Council of the European Union, 2011). Yet even without political cooperation, the EU may promote HEPA-friendly policies via EU-funded networks.

Table 3.6. HEPA projects co-financed in 2010-11

Project name, beneficiary, reference	Concept/idea	Partners
Consejería de los Jóvenes y del Deporte de la Junta de Extremadura (Regional Ministry for Youth and Sports of Extremadura): EAC/21/2009/203 – S2-PORT[27]	A project focussing on seniors (healthy ageing), aiming to develop a shared methodology for cross-sectoral collaboration in relation to HEPA and health referrals for seniors.	Regional Ministry for Youth and Sports of Extremadura (ES); University of Kent (UK); Pirkanmaan ammattikorkea a houlu OY-Dirkanmaan University of Applied Sciences Ltd. (FI); Active Institute (DK); Foundation for Research & Technology (GR); CONI Servizi Spa (IT); Observatory E-Medin (IT); as well as Business Development Friesland (NL).
Deutsche Sportjugend im Deutschen Olympischen Sportbund e.V., EAC/21/2009/033 – "Healthy Children in Sound Communit(ies)" (HCSC-EU)[28]	Building on the outcome and recommendations of the EU-funded study on "Young people's physical activities and sedentary lifestyles" (Brettschneider & Naul, 2005), and the subsequent follow-up in the "Healthy Children in Sound Communities" (HCSC) Interreg-funded project between Velen (DE) and Winterswijk (NL) (see Brettschneider, et al., 2009), the project is about building local, community-based, multi-actor networks, this time within a wider geographical framework (DE, NL, BE, CE, PL, IT, SE, UK).	Partners include a mixture of youth sport organisations, public authorities and academic institutions, ensuring a mixture of outreach and evaluation.

[27] http://ec.europa.eu/sport/calls-for-proposals/call2109/203_extremadura.pdf
[28] http://ec.europa.eu/sport/calls-for-proposals/call2109/033_dsdos.pdf

Diputació de Barcelona (Barcelona Provincial Council): EAC/21/2009/154 – "Euro Sport Health"[29]	Apart from a campaign in favour of sport for all provided by regional and local authorities, this project stood out by involving a peer-review exercise whereby examples of local good practice from the participating regions and cities were marked jointly. This was an impressive achievement, given that such a marking exercise would hardly be politically feasible at EU level, if based within official EU structures in Brussels. While the achievement of a Council-based monitoring mechanism regarding Member States' HEPA-relevant policies remains a priority for the Commission, marking would probably never be an option, as Governments do not enjoy being at the end of a league table. Yet as a peer exercise between regional and local authorities, it was obviously possible, and results are reported on the project website. This shows how EU funding can be a policy tool, even in the absence of EU-level recommendations.	Diputació de Barcelona (ES), Belfast City Council (UK), University of Castilla la Mancha, Research Group of sport facilities and organization management (ES), Budapest Association of Sports Federation (HU), Azienda USL della Valle d'Aosta (IT) and Cyprus Sports Organisation (CY).
European Health and Fitness Association (EHFA): EAC/21/2009/207 – "Becoming the Hub: The Health and Fitness Sector and the future of Health Enhancing Physical Activity"[30]	"The project will determine how the health and fitness sector can positively contribute to the drive to promote health-enhancing physical activity across the European Union through sport. It will identify and spread best practices across EHFA's pan-European network in the belief that the passion and expertise of exercise, fitness and sport professionals can be utilised as a major tool in the battle against sedentary lifestyles, ill health, obesity and social exclusion."	EHFA = an EU umbrella organisation, including fitness studio operators from the voluntary (non-profit), private (for-profit) and public sectors alike.

---

[29] http://ec.europa.eu/sport/calls-for-proposals/call2109/154_diba.pdf
[30] http://ec.europa.eu/sport/calls-for-proposals/call2109/207_ehfa.pdf

Fédération française d'athlétisme: EAC/21/2009/059 – ATHLE-SANTE[31]	"Mobilise diverse actors to contribute to HEPA for young, old, chronically ill and other interested people. The objective of the project is to create a network of health through sport." This time, a project led by a sport organisation, with only sport organisations participating, and always with the same sports discipline represented… Thus a totally different approach…	Partners: FAF (FR), FIDAL (IT), Real Federación Española de Atletismo (ES), Hungarian Athletics Association (HU), Deutscher Leichtathletik-Verband (D), European Athletics (CH).
International Sport and Culture Association (ISCA): EAC/21/2009/102 - SANTE (Sport Action Network of Europe)[32]	A network of sport-for-all organisations, with one municipality and some academic institutions…. "Best practises will be identified according to the following dimensions: Health-enhancing physical activity for specified target groups (seniors, youth, children); Health-enhancing physical activity in specific settings (sport clubs, kindergartens, schools); Health-enhancing physical activity methodologies and activity types (quality marks, campaigns, caravans); Health-enhancing physical activity partnerships (sport organisations vis-à-vis health institutions/hospitals, insurance companies, municipalities, patients' associations etc.)."	Partners: Czech Sport for All Association (CZ), DGI – Danish Gymnastics and Sport Associations (DK), Deutscher Turner-Bund (DTB) (DE), FEPI (BE), Federaziona Aerobico e Fitness- FIAF (IT), Foundation Inatel (PT), Latvian Sport for All Association (LV), Municipality of Florence (IT), Lithuanian country sport and culture association Nemunas (LT), Nederlandse Sport Alliantie (NL), Scottish Association of Local Sports Councils (SALSC) (UK), Czech Sokol Organization (CZ), Sports Unit of Slovenia (SI), UBAE (ES), UISP-Unione Italiana Sport Per Tutti (IT), Faculty of Sport Sciences, University of Cassino (IT).
Landeshauptstadt Stuttgart, Sportamt:	A network between big cities (compare this with the DSJ	Dimotiko Vrefomio Athinon, Athens

[31] http://ec.europa.eu/sport/calls-for-proposals/call2109/059_faf.pdf
[32] http://ec.europa.eu/sport/calls-for-proposals/call2109/102_isca.pdf

EAC/21/2009/126 – YOU NEED EXERCISE! Introducing every day Culture of Sports for Children in European Cities[33]	project) (big cities having other socio-cultural structures, determining sporta dn leisure haits, as well as food habits....): LEVEL 1: orientation to important sports political targets of the EU. LEVEL 2: identification of approved methods, development of innovative proposals, knowledge transfer among cities, development of common directives to encourage children to take exercise. LEVEL 3: higher number of network partners, comprehensive introduction of tried and tested methods within the EU, intensified utilisation of approved methods, inter-institutional knowledge transfer and within the institutions, orientation towards default 60 minutes exercise per day.	Municipal Creches and Childhood (GR); City of Copenhagen (DK); Innsbruck Stadt (AT); City of Rotterdam (NL); Landeshauptstadt Stuttgart (DE).
Suomen Kuntoliikuntaliitto (Kunto ry):EAC/21/2009/100 – SPORT CLUBS FOR HEALTH (SCFORH)[34]	Objectives: To develop advanced SCforH guidelines for European sport clubs; To establish a basis for a SCforH network in Europe. The project also aims to develop a cycle for the continuous development of the programme, to strengthen the responsible role of the national sports federations to motivate their member clubs to organise HEPA activities, to identify the role of the public sector as a supportive partner of SCforH programmes, to analyse the existing funding schemes and to develop advanced national funding systems, which support health-related physical activity promotion programs in sport clubs, and to operationalise the developed theoretical framework of the programme with the purpose of strengthening an	Kunto (sport-for-all organisation) (FI), Federazione Italiana Aerobica e Fitness – FIAF (IT), AccETTD- Cultural and Scientific Association of Tourism, Leisure and Sport (ES), Ministry of Sport and Tourism (PL), Estonian Sport for All Association (EE), Faculty of Kinesiology, University of Zagreb (Croatia).

[33] http://ec.europa.eu/sport/calls-for-proposals/call2109/126_landeshauptstadt.pdf
[34] http://ec.europa.eu/sport/calls-for-proposals/call2109/100_scforh.pdf

	evidence-based approach for the programme, providing a sound starting point for the evaluation of the programmes and opening to researchers possibilities to further study the field.	
World Health Organization (WHO), Regional Office for Europe, European Centre for Environment and Health: EAC/21/2009/067 – "NET-SPORT-HEALTH"[35]	*"Collection and content analysis of national sports promotion policies (identification of further national sport policies, upload of documents into an online database, refinement of existing policy document content analysis grid, translation of non-English documents into English, policy content analysis, international workshop, write summary and scientific paper). Support exchanges on health-enhancing physical activity (creation of a task force for the development of an HEPA Europe-EU Contact Group, establishment of regular exchange between the networks, session of the HEPA Europe – EU Contact Group at sixth annual meeting of HEPA Europe). Dissemination and communication (presentations at WHO meetings and other international events, website, print products and scientific publications, meetings of the WHO Counterparts on Physical Activity)."*	WHO, Palacky University, Olomouc, Czech Republic; All EU Member States.

---

[35] http://ec.europa.eu/sport/calls-for-proposals/call2109/067_who.pdf

3.5.2. Possibilities for incentive measures (funding)

EU funding is a soft policy tool of a particular kind, as financial instruments such as programmes have been created with political objectives in mind. By way of an example, follow-up to the Commission's ground-breaking study "Youth People's Lifestyle and Sedentariness" (Brettschneider & Naul, 2005) can be mentioned. This study, as mentioned above, started a process which led, among other things, to the adoption of non-binding EU Physical Activity Guidelines (European Commission, 2008). The political process, which included the creation of an EU Working Group Sport and Health in 2005, was flanked by at least one project which sought to follow up on key policy recommendations of the study (Brettschneider & Naul, 2005, Chapter 10, Recommendations, pp. 161-173), in particular as regards local multi-actor networks, to be linked across borders.

> "The complex cluster of sedentariness demands an intervention strategy which must be designed as an integrated approach of a multisectoral balanced network of different interventions linking the various settings in the living environment of children and adolescents: home, school, sport or social club, community. In order to establish such a // network and make it efficient for successful interventions new demands on policy and decision making are needed. They include further research, evaluation of the outcome and advocacy for changes of sedentary lifestyles." (Brettschneider & Naul, 2005, pp. 161-162)

As no actor can lift the challenge alone, local networks must be diverse. To test what works and what does not, given that local contexts vary while some factors may be assumed to remain invariable, EU networks are an ideal development tool. One bilateral project between a local authority in North-West Germany and one local authority in the Eastern Netherlands provided a direct follow-up and testing phase, establishing the "Healthy Children in Sound Communities" (HCSC) concept (Brettschneider, Hoffmann, Naul & Steinzen, 2009), in this case with EU funding from the Interreg programme. These experiences gained on a bilateral basis were later shared with a larger group of countries within the DSJ project among the nine HEPA projects co-financed by the Commission in 2010 (*Table 3.6;* see References, ref.: EAC/21/2009/033).[36] All nine projects were presented in detail at the EU Sport Forum in Budapest in February 2011, including detailed presentation in a large-scale workshop as well as stands in the exhibition area, both

---

[36] For hyperlinks permitting to access fact sheets as well as power point presentations explaining each of these nine projects, consult the section "Europe Commission (Sport Unit) documentation" in the References section.

designed to allow a maximum of networking and exchange of experiences and good practice (see References). Projects are expected to document their work in such a way as to permit the exhange of learning and exchange of good practice to take place even after they have ended, typically by making databases available on-line. In some cases, these databases are a corner stone of the project, while in others they are their very *raison d'être*. The WHO project "Net-Sport-Health", for example, illustrates the clearing-house function of EU-funded networks very clearly, as the project consisted largely in collecting, analysing, compiling and publishing national documents pertaining to sport and HEPA policies. To allow to a maximum snow-ball effect, the project led to the inclusion of HEPA-related information into a database already created with funding from the EU Public Health Programme, including national sport and HEPA-relevant legislation and policies (*Table 3.6;* see References, ref.: EAC/21/2009/069).

These projects were all so-called "preparatory actions", implying that they were intended to test the relevance of this type of EU funding as part of a future "sport chapter" within the "Erasmus for All" (ex-Life-Long Learning) programme. All preparatory actions of the years 2009-2010 have meanwhile undergone the required external evaluation and the final report submitted by the evaluators indicated that HEPA-type projects (having attracted 50% of the funding in 2009 and representing 50% of the projects co-financed under the budget of that year), together with the "social inclusion" projects, represented an area possibly deserving funding on a priority basis. Indeed, there,

> "[...] the Commission funded a relatively large number of projects (nine and five, respectively), while only two projects could be funded in gender equality. This doubtless reflects the enormity of HEPA and social inclusion-related problems and commensurate interest, which led to a large number of (high quality) proposals. In general, indicative and actual spend did not diverge heavily." (Economisti Associati, 2011, p. 68)

The last sentence is an indication that the projects were professionally run, including forecasts representing realistic and justified expectations as to the funding needed and the consumption rate expected. For those interested in EU-funded HEPA projects, the evaluation report contains encouraging messages:

> "It is recommended that the majority of funding for future incentive measures be dedicated to transnational networking projects, as these have shown the greatest potential for achieving EU added value across the range of priorities reflected in EU sport policy." (Economisti Associati, 2011, p. 84)

The evalution eport goes on to recommend allocating a minimum of €20m p.a. for HEPA projects in future EU budgets,

> "for achieving a critical mass of impacts cost effectively. This takes into account the magnitude of problems in specific subject areas, the absorption capacity of networks and the types of outcomes achieved during the years of Preparatory Action funding as well as the costs of administering incentive measures." (Economisti Associati, 2011, p. 84)

In consequence hereof, in its proposal for the Multiannual Financial Framework (MFF) 2014-2020, the Commission proposed a "sport chapter" as part of the future "Erasmus for All" programme (European Commission, 2011c). This would constitute a longical follow-up in relation to the Council's Work Plan on Sport 2011-2014 where HEPA is identified as one of the main themes flowing from the Commission's previous work (Council of the European Union, 2011, p. 4) – significantly, this gives HEPA (an "inspiration" topic) a status almost similar to such themes as free movement or match-fixing (established or potential "regulation" topics) – as one of the "social values of sport", alongside social inclusion, education and volunteering" (ibid., p. 5). As part of the Work Plan, an Expert Group "Sport, Health and Participation" was set up with the assigned task to "explore ways to promote health enhancing physical activity and participation in grassroot sport" (ibid., p. 10). The Work Plan also invited Member States and the Commission jointly (this being an area of so-called "shared competence") to:

> "promote better recognition of the contribution of sport to the overall goals of the Europe 2020 Strategy given the sector's strong potential to contribute to smart, sustainable and inclusive growth and new jobs and considering its positive effects on social inclusion, education and training as well as public health and active ageing" (Council of the European Union, 2011, p. 9).

These examples from the EU Work Plan show that EU funding is being used in a systematic way to further such values and objectives as have been (or will have been) defined, at the political level, as representing priorities for Europe. It is against this backdrop that EU funding for HEPA networks is to develop over the next years; it will have the opportunity to demonstrate the value and feasibility of alternative forms of cooperation and practice: in a sector which, in some Member States, may have a relatively conservative culture.

3.6. Conclusions

Europe needs action based on perspectives acknowledging that the steep increase in overweight cannot be attribute chiefly to some kind of "moral" weakness on the part of the individual: blaming the victim is a natural human reaction (cf., Montada & Lerner, 1998), and it can be expected to play a key role in shaping collective representations of overweight and obesity, yet as a political strategy it is utterly unhelpful. When societies go from a situation where overweight and obesity are marginal phenomena to one where they have become, statistically speaking, normal occurrences, and when this change has happened within just a few decades, then "shame and blame" strategies must be avoided, not only because they are intrinsically wrong due to the pain they inflict on other people, but also because they miss the point. This is why the "therapeutic trap" must be avoided, be it a clinical or a psycho-therapeutic one. If the lifestyle perspective is accepted, structural factors are important (ACSM, 2007; Troiano & Haskell, 2010) and structural factors driving unhealthy lifestyles must be identified, and guidance provided must go beyond the individual level ("30 min per day"). Even in the USA, with its long tradition for focussing on individual "failure," this has been recognised, at least in policy documents and research papers:

> "Provision of information alone, even scientifically-based physical activity guidelines, is not sufficient to bring about behavior change." (Troiano & Haskell, 2010, p. 38)

The EU has taken the logical step by adopting its Physical Activity Guidelines which go a step further, compared with WHO and US guidance, in defining the policies needed. But what kind of action should be taken?

Europe needs strategies for action involving as many sectors of society as possible, apt to capitalise on the vitality of its civil society in particular. While policy action based on the public health and consumer protection roles of the Union and its Member States is justified, policy action in the fields of sport and physical activity should be even more of a priority, since they allow for largely stigma-free, uncomplicated action, often at a surprisingly low investment cost.

Are sport and physical activity actors ready for the quantum leap embracing parameters that are not proper to their own sector? Are they ready to open up, not only conceptually but also in terms of diversifying their activities? This is strongly analogous to the quantum leap which the medical community once had to take in espousing social, cultural, geographical, cultural and other non-clinical aspects of health and ill-health. Although the medical community is still regularly portrayed by critical social scientists as being insensitive to non-somatic factors, social medicine took off as early as in the mid-19th century because some outstanding scholar-practitioners (in Germany: Virchow, Koch...) were prepared for this quantum leap and not afraid of going beyond the narrow confines of the sector within which they had received their professional socialisation. Following the 1848 typhus epidemic in Upper Silesia, the Prussian Government sent Rudolf Virchow (1821-1902) on a mission to investigate the effects of the epidemic clinically. Given his outstanding record of microscopy this must have seemed a safe bet. Yet Virchow did not limit himself to effects, he started looking for root causes, neither did he limit himself to the clinical aspects of the epidemic.

> "While there, Virchow came face-to-face with the destitute Polish minority, struggling in appalling circumstances. And so, instead of returning to Prussia with a set of strictly medical guidelines, Virchow's report recommended political change, plus sweeping educational and economic reforms. It was hardly what the government had bargained for."
> (Watson, 2010, p. 384)

And yet, this was not an activist or a sociologist on field work, but one of the greatest medical scholar-practitioners of the 19th century, one who had made, and continued to make ground-breaking discoveries with his microscope: one who even could not stay away from archaeology.

The academic and professional community of sport science, PE, etc., can and should make an important contribution in this regard, by showing to sports organisations and other civil society organisations what is possible in terms of HEPA practice; by develop pedagogical concepts to translate the most recent scientific knowledge into practice; and by mediating between the sport sectors, which sport scientists, PE teachers, etc., know well, and other sectors. As can be seen from the examples of the nine EU-funded HEPA projects presented above, this is a field where the EU can make a useful contribution – but one of inspiration rather than regulation.

Epilogue

> *"The EU's institutional agenda is very open and affords actors the opportunity to exploit a multiplicity of venues in order to influence policy."* (Parrish, 2003, p. 110)

> *"However, the EU's institutional agenda is very open. As an item for active policy consideration, sport has proved a relatively malleable item."* (ibid., p. 106)

The selected lectures included in this book (Chapters 1-3) were finalised around New Year's Day 2012 and represent the state of political developments and academic discussions at that time. Around New Year's Day 2012 they were collated to form this book, with the express aim to present the texts in the shape they had reached twelve months earlier. In the meantime, much of interest had happened at EU level. To name but a few:

- The EU was getting closer to a sport funding stream as part of a future education programme,[37] whether this will be known as "Erasmus 4 All" (E4A) (the Commission's proposal), YES Europe (Youth, Education & training, Sport) (Parliament's proposal)[38] or something else.

- The European Commission was getting closer to putting a HEPA-related policy proposal before the Council.[39]

- With the blessing of the American College of Sport Medicine (ACSM), European Initiative for Exercise is Medicine (EIEIM) was launched to promote HEPA values in the medical community.[40]

---

[37] See e.g., The proposal for an EU Programme for Education, Training, Youth and Sport: Introduction by the European Commission.
http://ec.europa.eu/sport/library/documents/b1/eusf2012-proposal-eu-prog-pv.pdf - See also: State of play at the European Parliament, MEP Santiago Fisas Ayxela. http://ec.europa.eu/sport/library/documents/b1/eusf2012-mep-santiago-fisas-ayxela.pdf

[38] Press Release – 27/11/2012 – YES Europe: EP names new programme for youth, education and sport. Doris Pack MEP.
http://www.eppgroup.eu/press/showpr.asp?prcontroldoctypeid=1&prcontrolid=11553&prcontentid=19210&prcontentlg=en

[39] See European Commission (2012): EU Physical Activity Guidelines: overview of progress. Last update: 03 July 2012. http://ec.europa.eu/sport/news/20120703-eu-pag-progress_en.htm

[40] See Press Release: International Experts Talked About Physical Activity and Exercise in Medicine. First Congress of EIEIM in Berlin from Oct 3 – 6, 2012.
http://s394973335.online.de/resources/Pressemitteilung2_Speakers.pdf

- The Council had delivered two "EU contributions" to WADA in view of the revision of the World Anti-Doping Code.[41]
- On 26-27 November 2012, the Council (Education, Culture, Youth, Sport) (EYCS) held a session which included as many as four different sport-related agenda items, all of them substantial: HEPA, sport statistics, anti-doping, match-fixing and proposals for a possible future Annual European Week of Sport.[42]
- In Belgium, the Flemish Community had given its Whereabouts system a thorough overhaul, thereby scaling down its Registered Testing Pool.[43]

These developments are all part of the wider picture, including EU-connected actions as well as dynamics unrelated to the EU. It would be mistaken to see "inspiration from Brussels" in every case involving themes which the EU has been involved in, yet the EU has become a sport policy actor and its agendas are also those of many other actors. The dynamics illustrated in this book continue unfolding themselves, with or without direct EU involvement: however, the examples listed above can all be expected to have been fostered to various degrees by action taken at EU level, and four out of six are actually EU-level initiatives, albeit such which are bound to depend upon active support and involvement from actors at other levels.

Sport-policy debates conducted at EU level will continue to be shaped under the influence of input from different actors with sometimes dissimilar agendas, whether open or hidden, as expressed in the two quotations from Parrish (2003) opening this Epilogue. The familiar mismatch – identified one decade ago in a seminal piece of scholarship – can be expected to continue featuring in the future, yet this does not diminish the EU's potential to provide inspiration as much as regulation.

---

[41] See Council approves EU contribution to the revision of the World Anti-Doping Code. Posted : 14 March 2012. http://ec.europa.eu/sport/news/20120314b_en.htm – See also: EU Council approves second EU contribution to the revision of the World Anti-Doping Code. Posted : 05 October 2012.
http://ec.europa.eu/sport/news/20121005-eu-council_en.htm

[42] See EU Council busy with sport issues: health, statistics, doping, match-fixing, possible European Week of Sport. Last update: 04 December 2012.
http://ec.europa.eu/sport/news/20121204-eu-council-sport-issues_en.htm

[43] See Muyters maakt whereabouts "klantvriendelijker", do 03/03/2011 - 10:23, http://www.sporza.be/cm/sporza/ander_nieuws/1.974510 – Compare with the older news item: •WADA: "Vlaanderen gaat te ver in dopingregels", 25/11/2010 – 08:52, http://www.sporza.be/cm/sporza/ander_nieuws/1.912330

The author intends to follow up on these and other developments in future papers devoted to the topics discussed in this book.

References

European Commission (Sport Unit) documentation

EU Working Group "Anti-Doping": http://ec.europa.eu/sport/library/consultation-and-co-operation_en.htm#antidoping

Expert Group "Anti-Doping":
http://ec.europa.eu/sport/library/consultation-and-co-operation_en.htm#xgad

13-15/05/2009 – Athens, EU Conference on Anti-Doping,
http://ec.europa.eu/sport/library/sport-and_en.htm

EAC/21/2009 Results of the selection process (HEPA projects co-financed from the 2009 Preparatory Action: http://ec.europa.eu/sport/preparatory_actions/results-eac-21-2009_en.htm

EAC/22/2010 Results of the selection process:
http://ec.europa.eu/sport/preparatory_actions/results-eac-22-2010_en.htm

21-22/02/2011 – Budapest – EU Sport Forum: First session: "2009 Preparatory Action in the field of sport":
http://ec.europa.eu/sport/library/consultation-and-co-operation_en.htm

Literature

Aagaard, M. (2007): EU vil sidestille dopingbagmænd med narkohandlere. In: Politiken, 12 July, p. 12

Abbott, A.D. (1988): The System of Professions: Essay on the Division of Expert Labour. Chicago: University of Chicago Press

ACSM [American College of Sports Medicine] & AHA [American Heart Association] (2007): Guidelines for healthy adults under age 65.
http://www.acsm.org/AM/Template.cfm?Section=Home_Page&TEMPLATE=CM/HTMLDisplay.cfm&CONTENTID=7764#Under_65

Anderson, J. (2010): Modern Sports Law: a Textbook. Oxford & Portland, Oregon: Hart Publishing

Article 29 Working Party (2008): Opinion 3/2008 of the Article 29 Working Party on the World Anti-Doping Code draft International Standard for the Protection of Privacy. 01.08.2008. WP 156.
http://ec.europa.eu/justice/policies/privacy/docs/wpdocs/2008/wp156_en.pdf

Article 29 Working Party (2009): Second opinion 4/2009 on the World Anti-Doping Agency (WADA) International Standard for the Protection of Privacy and Personal Information, on related provisions of the WADA Code and on other privacy issues in the context of the fight against doping in sport by WADA and (national) anti-doping organizations. 06.04.2009. WP 162.
http://ec.europa.eu/justice/policies/privacy/docs/wpdocs/2009/wp162_en.pdf

Bannenberg, B. & Rössner, D. (2006): Straftat gegen den Wettbewerb: Plädoyer für den Einsatz des Strafrechts bei Dopingverstößen. In: Weinreich, Jens (Hrsg.): Korruption im Sport. In: Weinreich, J. (ed): Korruption im Sport. Mafiose Dribblings, Organisiertes Schweigen. Leipzig: Forum Verlag, pp. 214-227

Barroso, M.A. (2011): Dopaje un negocio que mueve 15000 millones al año. In: ABC, 12.03.2011, http://www.abc.es/20110312/deportes/abci-dopaje-201103120320.html

Bay Nielsen, H.; Astrup, A.V.; Richelsen, B. & Kroustrup, J.P. (2006): Adipositas i Danmark: hvorfor er det ikke gået så galt? In: Ugeskrift for Læger, vol. 168, no. 2, pp. 132-135

Belet, I. (2009a): Question no 53 by Ivo Belet (H-0404/09). Subject: Combating doping – whereabouts.
http://www.europarl.europa.eu/sides/getDoc.do?pubRef=-//EP//TEXT+CRE+20091126
+ANN-01+DOC+XML+V0//EN&query=QUESTION&detail=H-2009-0404

Belet, I. (2009b): Vraag nr. 53 van Ivo Belet (H-0404/09). Betreft: Strijd tegen doping – whereabouts. http://www.europarl.europa.eu/sides/getDoc.do?pubRef=-//EP//TEXT+
CRE+20091126+ANN-01+DOC+XML+V0//NL&query=QUESTION&detail=H-2009-
0404

Berkey, C.S., Rockett, H.R., Field, A.E., Gillman, M.W., Frazier, A.L., & Camargo, C.A.J., et. al. (2000): Activity, Dietary Intake, and Weight Changes in a Longitudinal Study of Preadolescent and Adolescent Boys and Girls. In: Pediatrics, vol. 105, pp. E 56

Berne, E. (1964): Games People Play: the psychology of human relationships. New York: Grove Press

BBC (2008): Weight worry sees child in care. 19:32 GMT, Monday, 3 November 2008. http://news.bbc.co.uk/2/hi/uk_news/england/derbyshire/7707165.stm

BBC (2011): WADA: Criminal underworld controlling steroid trade. BBC, 16 March 2011

BBC Sport (2009): Legal threat to anti-doping code. Page last updated at 16:28 GMT, Thursday, 22 January 2009. http://news.bbc.co.uk/sport2/hi/front_page/7844918.stm

BMJ Editorial (2006): Pandemic obesity in Europe. In: British Medical Journal, vol. 333, no. 1081, 25.11., http://www.bmj.com/cgi/content/full/333/7578/1081

Bogni, R. (2010): The role of Eurobarometer surveys in the communication policy of the European Union. In: Studi sull'integrazione europea, vol. 5, no. 3, pp. 653-671

Booth, F.W.; Chakravarthy, M.V.; Gordon, S.E. & Spangenburg, E.E. (2002): Waging War on Physical Inactivity: using modern molecular ammunition against an ancient enemy. In: Journal of Applied Physiology, vol. 93, pp. 3-30

Bots, S.; Tijhuis, M.; Giampaoli, S.; Kromhout, D. & Nissinen, A. (2008): Lifestyle- and diet-related factors in late-life depression – a 5-year follow-up of elderly European men: the FINE study. In: International Journal of Geriatric Psychiatry, vol. 23, no. 5, pp. 478-484

Bouchard, C. (ed) (2000): Physical Activity and Obesity. Champaign, Ill.: Human Kinetics

Bozkurt, E. (2008): 18 december 2008 E-6778/08. SCHRIFTELIJKE VRAAG van Emine Bozkurt (PSE) aan de Commissie. Betreft: Aangepaste antidopingcode. http://www.europarl.europa.eu/sides/getDoc.do?pubRef=-//EP//TEXT+WQ+E-2008-6778+0+DOC+XML+V0//NL

Bray, E. (2011): The Curse of Good Hospitality: Why Developing Countries Shouldn't Host International Sporting Events. In: SAIS Review, vol. 31, no. 1, pp. 99-102

Brettschneider, W.D.; Hoffmann, D.; Naul, R. & Steinzen, A. (2009): Von den Erkenntnissen aus dem EU-Bericht „Young people's lifestyle and sedentariness" zur handlungsorientierten Umsetzung der Empfehlungen im Rahmen von zwei lokalen Präventionsstudien. In: Naul, R.; Krüger, A. & Schmidt, W. (eds): Kulturen des Jugendsports. Bildung, Erziehung und Gesundheit. Aachen: Meyer & Meyer, pp. 67-104

Brettschneider, W.D. & Naul, R. (2005): Study on young people's lifestyles and sedentariness and the role of sport in the context of education and as a means of restoring the balance. Paderborn: Universität Paderborn & Essen: Universität Duisburg-Essen. [Study commissioned by the European Commission.] http://ec.europa.eu/sport/library/doc/c1/doc374_en.pdf

Brettschneider, W.D. & Naul, R. (eds) (2007): Obesity in Europe: young people's physical activity and sedentary lifestyles. Frankfurt/Main: Peter Lang

Brown, A. (2007): IOC & FIFA: White Paper On Sport Is A 'Missed Opportunity'. In: World Sports Law Report, 11 July, http://www.e-comlaw.com/sportslawblog/template_permalink.asp?id=126

CAFDIS (undated): Concerted Action in the Fight against Doping in Sport (GTC1-2000-28002). http://ec.europa.eu/research/growth/gcc/projects/antidoping-cafdis.html

Callery, C. & McArdle, D. (2011): Doping, European law and the implications of Meca-Medina. In: International Journal of Sport Policy and Politics, vol. 3, no. 2, pp. 163-175

Carr-Saunders, A.M. & Wilson, P.A. (1933): The Professions. Oxford: Clarendon Press

CDC [Center for Disease Control] (1996): Physical activity and health: a report of the Surgeon General. Atlanta, GA: US Department of Health and Human Services, Center for Disease Control and Prevention

Chang, V.W. & Christakis, N.A. (2002): Medical modelling of obesity: a transition from action to experience in a 20th century American medical textbook. In: Sociology of Health & Illness, vol. 24, no. 2, pp. 151-177

Cohen, A. (2009): Tennis stars dispute doping ban. Breaking the 'whereabouts rule' three times leads to ban, even though there's no evidence. In: Wall Street Journal Europe, 24 December 2009

Council of the European Communities (1990): Resolution of 3 December 1990 on Community action to combat the use of drugs, including the abuse of medicinal products, particularly in sport. In: Official Journal of the European Communities, C 329, 31.12.1990, p. 2

Council of the European Communities (1992): Resolution of the Council and of the Representatives of the Member States, meeting within the Council on a code of conduct against doping in sport. In: Official Journal of the European Communities, C 44, 19.2.1992, pp. 1-2

Council of the European Union (2000): Conclusions of the Council and the Representatives of the Governments of the Member States, meeting within the Council of 4 December 2000 on combating doping. In: Official Journal of the European Union, C 356, 12.12.2000, p. 1

Council of the European Union (2008): Council Conclusions on a cooperation mechanism between the Council and the Commission for the implementation of the EU Health Strategy 2876th Employment, Social Policy, Health and Consumer Affairs Council meeting. Luxembourg, 10 June 2008
http://www.eu2008.si/en/News_and_Documents/Council_Conclusions/June/0609_EPSCO-Health_Strategy.pdf

Council of the European Union (2010): Conclusions of the Council and the Representatives of the Governments of the Member States, meeting within the Council, on the role of the EU in the international fight against doping. In: Official Journal of the European Union, C 324, 1.12.2010, p. 18

Council of the European Union (2011a): Resolution of the Council and of the Representatives of the Governments of the Member States, meeting within the Council, on a European Union Work Plan for Sport for 2011-2014. In: Official Journal of the European Union, C 162, 1.6.2011, pp. 1-5

Council of the European Union (2011b): Resolution of the Council and the Representatives of the Governments of the Member States, meeting within the Council on the representation of the EU Member States in the Foundation Board of WADA and the coordination of the EU and its Member States' positions prior to WADA meetings. In: Official Journal of the European Union, C 372, 20.12.2011, pp. 7-9

Crum, A.J. & Langer, E.J. (2007): Mind-Set Matters: Exercise and the Placebo Effect. In: Psychological Science, vol. 18, no. 2, pp. 165-171

D'Amario, R. & Froidmont-Görtz, I. de (2005): The Fight against Obesity: examples of EU projects in the field of nutrition and obesity.European Union. European Commission. Directorate-General for Research. Luxembourg : EUR-OP (EUR 21718)

Darnton, P. (2009): A health revolution: the role of cycling in the UK's public health challenges. In: ph. com - The newsletter of the Faculty of Public Health, June, p. 13, http://www.fph.org.uk/uploads/phcom_Jun09.pdf

Die Zeit (2011a): Bundesarbeitsgericht bestätigt Sonderrecht für Kirchen. In: Die Zeit, 8.9.2011, http://www.zeit.de/karriere/beruf/2011-09/urteil-bag-kirche-mitarbeiter

Die Zeit (2011b): Papst mahnt zur Aufgabe von kirchlichen Privilegien. In: Die Zeit, 25.9.2011,
http://www.zeit.de/gesellschaft/zeitgeschehen/2011-09/papst-freiburg-konzerthaus

Dikic, N.; Samardzic-Markovic, S. & McNamee, M. (2011): On the Efficacy of WADA's Whereabouts Policy: between filing failures and missed tests. In: Deutsche Zeitschrift für Sportmedizin, vol. 62, no. 10, pp. 324- 328, http://www.zeitschrift-sportmedizin.de/fileadmin/externe_websites/ext.dzsm/content/archiv 2011/heft10/online_10_11/324_originalia_dikic.pdf

Donaldson, L. (2009): Evidence for the health benefits of physical activity. In: ph. com – The newsletter of the Faculty of Public Health, June, p. 1, http://www.fph.org.uk/uploads/phcom_Jun09.pdf

DR Sporten (2010): Formand gik enegang i fyring af dopingchef. 01. nov. 2010 12.11 Doping. http://www.dr.dk/Sporten/Oevrig_sport/Doping/2010/11/01/120903.htm

Duijvenbode, D.C. van; Hoozemans, M.J.M.; Poppel, M.N.M. & van Proper, K.I. (2009): The relationship between overweight and obesity, and sick leave: a systematic review. International Journal of Obesity, vol. 33, no. 8, pp. 807-816

EHFA [European Health and Fitness Association] (2011): Fitness Against Doping. Interim Report. 8th November 2011. http://www.ehfa-programmes.eu/files/FAD%20-%20Web%20Interim%20Report%20Nov_11.pdf

Economisti Associati srl; The Evaluation Partnership; navreme Boheme; SCIENTER; Amitié & Ipsos-MORI (2011): Framework Contract EAC/50/2009 Framework Contract for Evaluation, Evaluation Related Services and Support for Impact Assessment. Specific Contract: Evaluation of Preparatory Actions and special events in the field of sport. Final Report of the Evaluation. 17 July 2011. http://ec.europa.eu/sport/news/doc/evaluation_final_report_prepact_special_events_20110727.pdf

Eichberg, H. (2004): The People of Democracy.Understanding Self-Determination on the Basis of Body and Movement. Aarhus (Denmark): Klim (ISCA Movement Studies, vol. 5)

EU Athletes (2003): Collective Labor Agreement "Professional Players 2003". http://www.euathletes.info/uploads/media/AccColl_2oIngleseSerieA_copy.pdf

European Commission (1999): Communication: Community support plan to combat doping in sport. COM(1999) 643, 1.12.2009, http://eur-lex.europa.eu/LexUriServ/LexUriServ.do?uri=COM:1999:0643:FIN:EN:PDF

European Commission (2005): Communication [...]: The EU action in the field of Education through Sport: building on EYES 2004 achievements. COM(2005) 680, 22.12.2005. http://eur-lex.europa.eu/LexUriServ/site/en/com/2005/com2005_0680en01.pdf

European Commission (2007a): White Paper on A Strategy for Europe on Nutrition, Overweight and Obesity related health issues. COM(2007) 279, 30.05.2007. http://eur-lex.europa.eu/LexUriServ/site/en/com/2007/com2007_0279en01.pdf

European Commission (2007b): White Paper on Sport. COM (2007) 391, 11.07.2007. http://ec.europa.eu/sport/white-paper/index_en.htm

European Commission (2007c): White Paper: Together for Health: A Strategic Approach for the EU 2008-2013. Brussels, 23.10.2007, COM(2007) 630 final.
http://ec.europa.eu/health-eu/doc/whitepaper_en.pdf

European Commission (2008a): Brussels, 10 October 2008. EU Physical Activity Guidelines: Recommended Policy Actions in Support of Health-Enhancing Physical Activity. Approved by the EU Working Group "Sport & Health" at its meeting on 25 September 2008. Confirmed by EU Member State Sport Ministers at their meeting in Biarritz on 27-28 November 2008
http://ec.europa.eu/sport/library/doc/c1/pa_guidelines_4th_consolidated_draft_en.pdf

European Commission (2008b): Questions and Answers on criminal law measures against maritime pollution. MEMO/08/156. Brussels, 11 March 2008
http://europa.eu/rapid/pressReleasesAction.do?reference=MEMO/08/156&format=HTML&aged=1&language=EN&guiLanguage=en

European Commission (2009a): 39471 Certain joueur de tennis professionnel / Agence mondiale antidopage + ATP + CIAS. Case COMP/39.471) Bruxelles, 12.10.2009, SG-Greffe(2009) D/6632, C(2009)7809,
http://ec.europa.eu/competition/antitrust/cases/dec_docs/39471/39471_146_5.pdf

European Commission (2009b): EU Conference on Anti-Doping – Organised by the European Commission – Athens, Greece, 13-15 May 2009 – Michal Krejsa, Head of the Sport Unit, European Commission: Criminalisation of Trade in Doping Substances. http://ec.europa.eu/sport/library/doc/c2/michal_krejsa_speech.pdf

European Commission (2011a): Communication from the Commission to the European Parliament, the Council, the Economic and Social Committee and the Committee of the Regions: Developing the European Dimension in Sport. Brussels, 18.1.2011, COM(2011) 12 final. (See: http://ec.europa.eu/sport/news/news984_en.htm)

European Commission (2011b): Impact Assessment: Accompanying document to the Communication from the Commission to the European Parliament, the Council, the Economic and Social Committee and the Committee of the Regions: Developing the European Dimension in Sport. Brussels, 18.1.2011, SEC(2011) 67 final. (See: http://ec.europa.eu/sport/news/news984_en.htm)

European Commission (2011c): Communication: A Budget for Europe 2020, 29.6.2011, COM(2011) 500. http://europa.eu/press_room/pdf/a_budget_for_europe_2020_en.pdf

European Commission (2012): Reform of data protection legislation. Last update: 25/01/2012. http://ec.europa.eu/justice/data-protection/index_en.htm

European Council (1998): Vienna European Council 11 and 12 December 1998: Please Conclusions. XII – Sport. http://www.europarl.europa.eu/summits/wie1_en.htm#12

European Opinion Research Group EEIG (2003a): Eurobaromtère spécial 197 / Vague 60.0 - European Opinion Research Group EEIG: Les citoyens de l'Union européenne et le sport. http://ec.europa.eu/public_opinion/archives/ebs/ebs_197_fr_summ.pdf

European Opinion Research Group EEIG (2003b): Special Eurobarometer 183-6 / Wave 58.2: Physical Activity. Brussels: European Commission.
http://ec.europa.eu/public_opinion/archives/ebs/ebs_183_6_en.pdf

European Parliament (2005): European Parliament Resolution on combating doping in sport, 16 March 2005, PE 356.381v01-00, B6-0215/2015, http://www.europarl.europa.eu/sides/getDoc.do?type=MOTION&reference=B6-2005-0215&language=EN

European Parliament (2011a): Opinion of the Committee on Civil Liberties, Justice and Home Affairs (3.10.2011) for the Committee on Culture and Education on the European dimension in sport (2011/2087(INI)). Rapporteur: Emine Bozkurt.
http://www.europarl.europa.eu/sides/getDoc.do?type=REPORT&reference=A7-2011-0385&language=EN#title7

European Parliament (2011b): Report on a comprehensive approach on personal data protection in the European Union (2011/2025(INI)). Committee on Civil Liberties, Justice and Home Affairs. Rapporteur: Axel Voss. 22 June 2011. PE 460.636v02-00, A7-0244/2011,
http://www.europarl.europa.eu/sides/getDoc.do?type=REPORT&reference=A7-2011-0244& language=EN

European Parliament, Directorate General Internal Policies of the Union, Policy Department Structural and Cohesion Policies (2008): Doping in Professional Sport: Study: Summary. IP/B/CULT/IC/2007-067. PE 409.356. Brussels: European Parliament. http://www.europarl.europa.eu/meetdocs/2004_2009/documents/dv/729/729977/7299 77en.pdf

Fertel, A.K. (2007): Doping and the Presumption of Guilt: Everybody Loses. In: Sports Litigation Alert Archives, April 13,
http://www.hackneypublications.com/sla/archive/000451.php

Figel', J. (2009): EU Conference on Anti-Doping – Organised by the European Commission – Athens, Greece, Wednesday, 13 May to Friday, 15 May 2009: Video Message Commissioner Figel'.
http://ec.europa.eu/sport/library/doc/c2/video_message_jf_text.pdf

Figura, L. (2009): Doping: zwischen Freiheitsrecht und notwendigem Verbot. Aachen: Meyer & Meyer Verlag (Sportforum, Bd. 20)

Focus (2009): 26.11.2009 Eisschnelllauf National: Doping-Experte: „Urteil erzeugt Unwohlsein". http://www.focus.de/sport/wintersport/eisschnelllauf-doping-experte-urteil-erzeugt-unwohlsein_aid_457743.html

FIFA (2007): EU White Paper on Sport: Much work remains to be done (FIFA.com) Wednesday 11 July 2007.
http://www.fifa.com/aboutfifa/federation/releases/newsid=550327.html#eu+white+p aper+sport+much+work+remains+done

Flexner, A. [1915] (2001): "Is Social Work a Profession?" [Paper presented at the National Conference on Charities and Correction, 1915]. Reprinted in: Research on Social Work Practice, vol. 11, no. 2, pp. 152-165

Freidson, E. (1986): Professional Powers: a study of the institutionalization of formal knowledge. Chicago: University of Chicago Press

García [García], B. (2007): UEFA and the European Union, from confrontation to co-operation?. In: Journal of Contemporary European Research, J. 3, H. 3, S. 202-223

García García, B. (2008): The European Union and the Governance of Football: a Game of Levels and Agendas. A Doctoral thesis. Submitted in partial fulfilment of the requirements for the award of Doctor of Philosophy of Loughborough University. Loughborough University Institutional Repository. http://hdl.handle.net/2134/5609

GHK (2010): Volunteering in the European Union, final report, http://ec.europa.eu/citizenship/eyv2011/doc/Volunteering%20in%20the%20EU%20Final%20Report.pdf

Green, M. (2006): From 'Sport for All' to Not About 'Sport' at All?: Interrogating Sport Policy Interventions in the United Kingdom. In: European Sport Management Quarterly, vol. 6, no. 3, pp. 217-238

Groll, M. (2005): Transnationale Sportpolitik. Analyse und Steuerungsansatz sportpolitischer Interaktionen. Aachen: Meyer & Meyer Verlag (Sportforum, Bd. 14)

Groll, M.; Gütt, M. & Mittag, J. (2008): Political aspects of sport in the European Union. Status Report within the framework of the project "Sport in Europe – Social, Political, Organisational, Legal Transparency in Europe". Cologne: German Sport University Cologne [Deutsche Sporthochschule]. Institute of European Sport Development and Leisure Studies.
http://www.sport-in-europe.eu/images/stories/PDFFiles/politische%20aspekte_final_end_1201.pdf

Grupe, O. (1984): Grundlagen der Sportpädagogik: Körperlichkeit, Bewegung u. Erfahrung im Sport. 3. Aufl. Schorndorf: Hofmann (Wissenschaftliche Schriftenreihe des Deutschen Sportbundes, vol. 8)

Hansen, K.C.; Zhang, Z.; Gomez, T.; Adams, A.K. & Schoeller, D.A. (2007): Exercise increases the proportion of fat utilization during short-term consumption of a high-fat diet. In: American Journal of Clinical Nutrition, vol. 85, pp. 109-116

Hanstad, D.V. & Loland, S. (2009): Elite athletes' duty to provide information on there whereabouts: justifiable anti-doping work or an indefensible surveillance system? In: European Journal of Sport Science, vol. 9, no. 1, pp. 3-10

HARDOP (undated): Harmonisation of Methods and Measurements in the Fight against doping (HARDOP). Final Report. Project SMT4-1998-6530.
http://ec.europa.eu/research/smt/hardop-en.pdf

Hatje, A. (2001): Loyalität als Rechtsprinzip in der Europäischen Union. Baden-Baden: Nomos (Schriftenreihe Europäisches Recht, Politik und Wirtschaft, vol. 262)

Heinonen, T.; Metteri, A. & Leach, J. (2009): Applying health determinants and dimensions in social work practice. In: European Journal of Social Work, vol. 12, no. 2, pp. 139-153

Higham, P. (2009): Options against Obesity. In: Professional Social Work: Magazine of the British Association of Social Workers (BASW), March, pp. 26-27

Hlobil, H.; Uegaki, K.; Staal, B.J.; Bruyne, M.C. de; Smid, T. & Mechelen, W. van (2005): Substantial sick-leave costs savings due to a graded activity intervention for workers with non-specific sub-acute low back pain. In: European Spine Journal, vol. 16, p. 919-924

HLN (2010): "Nog iets meer dan 5 procent Vlamingen in Brussel", 03/09/10 04u09 http://www.hln.be/hln/nl/957/Belgie/article/detail/1152830/2010/09/03/Nog-iets-meer-dan-5-procent-Vlamingen-in-Brussel.dhtml

H.M. Government (2009): Be active, be healthy. A plan for getting the nation moving. London: H.M. Government, Department of Health. http://www.dh.gov.uk/prod_consum_dh/groups/dh_digitalassets/documents/digitalas set/dh_094359.pdf

Hardman, K. (2002): Context for sport and physical education in Germany. In: Hardman, K. & Naul, R. (eds): Sport and Physical Education in Germany. London & New York: Routledge, pp. 1-14

Herrmann, P. (2009): Die Europäische Union als Programmgesellschaft. Das Europäische Gesellschaftsmodell, die Sozialpolitik und der Dritte Sektor Bremen: Europäischer Hochschulverlag

Höfer, A. (2008): Die Olympische Idee: Europäisches Erbe, globale Perspektive. In: Klöpsch, V.; Lämmer, M. & Tokarski, W. (eds): Sport in China. Beiträge aus interdisziplinärer Sicht. Köln: Sportverlag Strauß (Veröffentlichungen der Deutschen Sporthochschule Köln, vol. 16), pp. 173-181

Houlihan, B. (2006): Civil rights, doping control and the World Anti-Doping Code. In: Giulianotti, R. & McArdle, D. (eds): Sport, Civil Liberties and Human Rights. London: Routledge, pp. 128-145 (Cited: Waddington, 2010)

Huizinga, J. [1938] (1962): Homo ludens. Vom Ursprung der Kultur im Spiel. Reinbeck bei Hamburg: Rowohlt (Rowohlts Deutsche Enzyoklpädie, vol. 21)

Iapetos Consulting (2003): Evaluation of pilot projects co-financed by the European Commission in the field of the fight against doping. http://ec.europa.eu/sport/library/doc/c2/doc368_en.pdf

Ilešič, M. (2010): The Development of the Law and the Practice in the Post-Bosman Era. In: Poiares Maduro, M.P. & Azoulai, L. (eds): The Classics of EU Law Revisited on the 50th Anniversary of the Rome Treaty 2010. Oxford & Portland, Oregon: Hart Publishing, S. 477-479

Infantino, G. & Mavroidis, P.C. (2010): Inherit the Wind: A Comment on the Bosman Jurisprudence. In: Poiares Maduro, M.P. & Azoulai, L. (eds): The Classics of EU Law Revisited on the 50th Anniversary of the Rome Treaty 2010. Oxford & Portland, Oregon: Hart Publishing, pp. 498-505

ISCA [International Sport and Culture Association] (2011): 15/4/2011. 2010 Declaration on grassroots sports and citizenship. http://www.isca-web.org/english/news/2010declarationongrassrootsportsand citizenship

Jakicic, J.M.; Clark, K.; Coleman, E.; Donnelly, J.E.; Foreyt, J & Melanson, E. (2001): ACSM position stand: Appropriate intervention strategies for weight loss and prevention of weight regain for adults. In: Medicine and Science in Sports and Exercise, vol. 33, pp. 2145-2156

James, W.P.T. (2008): WHO recognition of the global obesity epidemic. In: International Journal of Obesity, vol. 32, no. S7, pp. S120-S126

Jesse, B. & Fischer, C. (2010): Sportstrukturen der Länder der Europäischen Union. In: Tokarski, W. & Petry, K. (eds): Handbuch Sportpolitik. Schorndorf: Hofmann Verlag, pp. 114-127

Johnson, T. (1972): Professions and Power. London: Heinemann

Joos, G. & Scheurle, K.D. (1989): Die bundesstaatliche Ordnung im Integrationsprozess unter besonderer Berücksichtigung der EuGH-Rechtsprechung und der Rechtsschutzmöglichkeiten der Länder. In: Europarecht, vol. 24, no. 3, pp. 226-236

Kamann, M. (2011): Gar nicht christlich. Ver.di kritisiert die Kirche als Arbeitgeber und fordert die Abschaffung des Streikverbots in der evangelischen Diakonie. In: Die Welt, 5. November, p. 10

Klabbers, J. (2008): Treaty Conflict and the European Union. Cambridge: Cambridge University Press

Klöpsch, V.; Lämmer, M. & Tokarski, W. (2008): Vorwort. In: Klöpsch, V.; Lämmer, M. & Tokarski, W. (eds): Sport in China. Beiträge aus interdisziplinärer Sicht. Köln: Sportverlag Strauß (Veröffentlichungen der Deutschen Sporthochschule Köln, vol. 16), pp. 5-7

König, W. (1993): Der zukünftige europäische Binnenmarkt und die Konsequenzen für den Sport. In: Tokarski, W.; Triphaus, L. & Petry, K. (eds): Der Sport im Der Sport im zusammenwachsenden Europa. Sportpolitische und sportfachliche Aspekte. Köln: Sport und Buch Strauß (Veröffentlichungen der Deutschen Sporthochschule Köln, vol. 11), pp. 17-36

Kornbeck, J. (2006a): Governance als Soft Law: Innovation oder Notwendigkeit im sportpolitischen Handeln der EU? In: Tokarski, W.; Petry, K. & Jesse, B. (eds): Sportpolitik. Theorie- und Praxisfelder von Governance im Sport. Cologne: Sportverlag Strauß (Veröffentlichungen der Deutschen Sporthochschule Köln, vol. 15), pp. 31-52

Kornbeck, J. (2006b): Sport und EG/EU – Ein horizontales oder vertikales Thema? Eine Zwischenbilanz der ersten dreißig Jahre (1974-2004). In: Sport und Gesellschaft / Sport and Society, vol. 3, no. 1, pp. 81-103

Kornbeck, J. (2007): Social Work Academics as Humboldtian Researcher-Educators: discussion of a survey of staff profiles from schools in Denmark, England and Germany. In: Social Work Education, vol. 26, no. 1, pp. 86-100

Kornbeck, J. (2008): Anti-Doping in and beyond the European Commission's White Paper on Sport. In: International Sports Law Journal, vol. 2008, no. 3-4, pp. 30-35

Kornbeck, J. (2009a): More than a Nutrition Issue: assessing the capacity of the EU to use physical activity and sport to counteract obesity. In: Westerbeek, Hans (ed): Using Sport to advance Community Health: an international perspective. Nieuwegein: Arko Sports Media (Ministerie van Volksgezondheid, Welzijn en Sport), pp. 153-174

Kornbeck, J. (2009b): Sozialpädagogische Adipositasbewältigung zwischen Psychotherapie und Bewegungsförderung. In: Theorie und Praxis der Sozialen Arbeit, vol. 60, no. 1, pp. 28-33

Kornbeck, J. (2009c): Why Social Work Can't Ignore Obesity. In: Professional Social Work: Magazine of the British Association of Social Workers (BASW), February, pp. 21-22

Kornbeck, J. (2010): Dopingbekämpfung: Harmonisierungspotential durch die EU nach Inkrafttreten des Vertrags von Lissabon? In: Monatsschrift für Kriminologie und Strafrechtsreform, vol. 93, no. 3, pp. 198-213

Kornbeck, J. (2011): Wozu Dopingbekämpfung in „dürftiger Zeit?" In: Buschmann, J.; Lämmer, M. & Petry, K. (eds): Internationale Aspekte und Perspektiven des Sports. Prof. Dr. Walter Tokarski zum 65. Geburtstag. Sankt Augustin: Academia Verlag, pp. 131-150

Krüger, A. (2008): Grundlagen der Doping-Prophylaxe. In: Kauerhof, R.; Nagel, S. & Zebisch, M. (Hrsg.): Doping und Gewaltprävention. Dokumentation des Leipziger Sportrechtstages 2007. Leipzig: Leipziger Universitätsverlag, pp. 143-166

Krustrup, P.; Nielsen, J.J.; Krustrup, B.R.; Christensen, J.F.; Pedersen, H.; Randers, M.B.; Aagaard, P.; Petersen, A.M. ; Nybo, L. & Bangsbo, J. (2009): Recreational soccer is an effective health-promoting activity for untrained men. In: British Journal of Sports Medicine, vol. 43, pp. 825-831

Ladenburger, C. (2008): Police and Criminal Law in the Treaty of Lisbon: A New Dimension for the Community Method. In: European Constitutional Law Review, vol. 4, pp. 20-40

La Libre Belgique (2009): Belgian tennis players appeal doping bans. November 18, 2009. http://www.wtop.com/?nid=237&sid=1816213

Lamfalussy, C. (2010): 5,3 % de Flamands à Bruxelles. Mis en ligne le 03/09/2010. http://www.lalibre.be/actu/belgique/article/606798/53-de-flamands-a-bruxelles.html

Lang, T. & Rayner, G. (2005): Obesity: a growing issue for European policy? In: Journal of European Social Policy 2005, vol. 15, no. 4, pp. 301-327

Larsen, K. & og Brinkkjær, U. (2008): Om Statsautoriseret normalisering af kroppe – BMI, professioner og sundhedskanon. In: Dansk pædagogisk Tidsskrift, vol. 2008, no. 3, pp. 42-49

Leach, K. (2006): The Overweight Patient A Psychological Approach to Understanding and Working with Obesity. London: Jessica Kingsley Publishers

Leedy, G. (2009): "I can't cry and run at the same time": women's use of distance running. In: Affilia: Journal of Women and Social Work, vol. 24, no. 1, pp. 80-93

Lombard, D. (2009): GSCC dismisses chief executive Mike Wardle. Rosie Varley: new chief executive and directors will have 'greater clarity of purpose'. In: Community Care, Monday 09 November 2009 12:02. http://www.communitycare.co.uk/Articles/2009/11/09/113111/gscc-dismisses-chief-executive-mike-wardle.htm

López, B. (2012): Doping as technology: a rereading of the history of performance-enhancing substance use in the light of Brian Winston's interpretative model for technological continuity and change. In: International Journal of Sport Policy and Politics, vol. 4, issue 1, pp. 55-71, advance access: DOI: 10.1080/19406940.2011.627361

Marks, G. (1993): Structural policy and Multi-level governance in the EC. In: Cafruny, A. & and Rosenthal, G. (eds): The State of the European Community: The Maastricht Debate and Beyond. Boulder, CO: Lynne Rienner, pp. 391-411

Martin, B. (2010): Prospects for promoting physical activity among children. (Physical Activity and Health Work Unit, Institute for Social and Preventive Medicine, University of Zurich). Presentation at the "Cities for Sport" conference. Stuttgart, 01.10.2010. http://www.citiesforsports.eu/project/conference/presentations.html

Mavrommatis, M. (2008): 2008E-2049/08: Written Question by Manolis Mavrommatis (PPE-DE) to the Commission. Subject: European Anti-Doping Agency: http://www.europarl.europa.eu/sides/getDoc.do?pubRef=-//EP//TEXT+WQ+E-2008-2049+0+DOC+XML+Vo//EN&language=MT

Merkur (2008): Neues Bürokratie-Monster aus Brüssel? In: Merkur, 05.08.08, http://www.merkur-online.de/nachrichten/politik/neues-buerokratie-monster-bruessel-88982.html

Merton, R.K. (1995): The Thomas Theorem and the Matthew Effect. In: Social Forces, vol. 74, no. 2, pp. 379-424

Mittag, J. (2011): Vergessene Kapitel europäischer Integrations- und Sportentwicklung: die Spiele europäischer Auswahlmannschaften. In: Buschmann, J.; Lämmer, M. & Petry, K. (eds): Internationale Aspekte und Perspektiven des Sports. Prof. Dr. Walter Tokarski zum 65. Geburtstag. Sankt Augustin: Academia Verlag, pp. 161-177

Mittag, J. & Groll, M. (2010): Theoretische Ansätze zur Analyse europäischer und transnationaler Sportpolitik und Sportstrukturen. In: Tokarski, W. & Petry, K. (eds): Handbuch Sportpolitk. Schorndorf: Hofmann (Beiträge zur Lehre und Forschung im Sport, Bd. 172), pp. 29-46

Møller, V. (2010): The Ethics of Doping and Anti-Doping: redeeming the soul of sport. London, et al.: Routledge

Montada, L. & Lerner, M. (eds) (1998): Responses to victimizations and belief in the just world. New York: Plenum

Morris, J.N.; Heady, J.A.; Raffle, P.A.B.; Roberts, C.G. & Parks, J.W. (1953): Coronary heart disease and physical activity of work. In: The Lancet, vol. 262, no. 6796, 28.11., pp. 1111-1120

Mostyn, P. (2006): Treatment of Psychosexual Problems. In: Henderson, C.; Smith, C.; Smith, S. & Stevens, A. (eds): Women and Psychiatric Treatment: a comprehensive text and practical guide. London & New York: Routledge, pp. 213-227

Nabokov, V. (1984): Lectures on Don Quixote. Edited by Fredson Bowers. Foreword by Guy Davenport. San Diego, et al.: Harvest Harcourt

Naul, R. & Holze, J. (2011): Sports Development and Young People: the role of international organizations. In: Houlihan, B. & Green, M. (eds): Routledge Handbook of Sports Development. London& New York: Routledge, pp. 198-211

Niedersächsisches Innenministerium (2001): Dopingbekämpfung in kommerziell geführten Fitnessstudios. http://ec.europa.eu/sport/library/doc/c2/doc362_en.pdf

Oja, P.; Bull, F.C.; Fogelholm, M. & Martin, B.W. (2010): Physical activity recommendations for health: what should Europe do? In: BMC Public Health, vol. 10, no. 10, http://www.biomedcentral.com/1471-2458/10/10

Overman, S.J. (2011): The Protestant Ethic and the Spirit of Sport: How Calvinism and Capitalism Shaped America's Games. Macon, GA: Mercer University Press

Owen, N.; Healy, G.N.; Matthews, C.E. & Dunstan, D.W. (2010): Too much sitting: the population health science of sedentary behavior. In: Exercise and Sport Science Reviews, vol. 38, no. 3, pp. 105-113

Pappous, A. (2011): Do the Olympic Games lead to a sustainable increase in grass roots sport participation?: a secondary analysis of Athens 2004. In: Savery, I.J. & Gilbert, K. (eds): Sustainability and Sport. Champaign, Illinois: Common Ground Publishing, pp. 81-87.

Parensen, A. (1998): Die Fussball-Bundesliga und das Bosman-Urteil. In: Tokarski, W. (ed): EU-Recht und Sport. Aachen: Meyer & Meyer, pp. 70-150

Parisi, P. (2007): Health, Development and Education in an Integral Perspective. In: Brettschneider, W.D. & Naul, R. (eds): Obesity in Europe: young people's physical acivity and sedentary lifestyles. Frankfurt/Main: Peter Lang, pp. 101-118

Parrish, R. (2003): Sports Law and Policy in the European Union. Manchester: Manchester University Press

Parry, R. (2008): Seven obese kids taken into care. 29/10/2008.
http://www.mirror.co.uk/news/top-stories/2008/10/29/seven-obese-kids-taken-into-care-115875-20849466/

Peers, S. (2008): EU Criminal Law and the Treaty of Lisbon. In: European Law Review, vol. 33, no. 4, pp. 507-529

Petry, K.; Froberg, K.; Madella, A. & Tokarski, W. (eds) (2008): Higher Education in Sport in Europe: from labour market demand to training supply. Aachen: Meyer & Meyer

Pieth, M. (2012): Sportverbände dürfen kein Freiraum für Geschäftemacher sein. In: Die Zeit, 01.02.2012 - 11:28 Uhr, http://www.zeit.de/sport/2012-02/fifa-korruption-pieth-sport-blatter

Poiares Maduro, M.P. & Azoulai, L. (Hrsg.): The Classics of EU Law Revisited on the 50th Anniversary of the Rome Treaty 2010. Oxford & Portland, Oregon: Hart Publishing

Polednak A.P. (1976): College athletes, body size, and cancer mortality. In: Cancer, vol. 38, pp. 382-387

Prozorov, S. (2004): Political Pedagogy of Technical Assistance: A Study in Historical Ontology of Russian Postcommunism. Tampere: Tampere University Press (Studia Politica Tamperensis, no. 11; Acta Electronica Universitatis Tamperensis, no. 310), http://acta.uta.fi/pdf/951-44-5847-8.pdf

Puhl, R.; Wharton, C. & Heuer, C. (2009): Weight Bias among Dietetics Students: Implications for Treatment Practices. In: Journal of the American Dietetic Association, vol. 109, no. 3, pp. 438-444

Ram, H. (2009): Democratic values and the global fight against doping. Paper presented at the Play the Game Conference. June, Coventry. (Cited: Waddington, 2010)

Reuters (2007): Fat Spanish boy taken into care.
http://www.reuters.com/news/video?videoId=47236

Rosamond, B. (2000): Theories of European Integration. Houndsmilss: Palgrave Macmillan

Robinson, N. (2007): More than a Regulatory State: bringing expenditure (back) into EU research / Nick Robinson. In: Comparative European Politics, vol. 5, no. 2, pp. 179-204

Röthel, A. (2000): Kompetenzen der Europäischen Union zur Dopingbekämpfung. In: Röhricht, V. & Vieweg, K. (Hrsg.): Doping-Forum. Aktuelle rechtliche und medizinische Aspekte. Stuttgart (Cited: Figura, 2009)

Rütten, A. & Abu-Omar, K. (2004): Prevalence of physical activity in the European Union. In: Sozial- und Präventivmedizin/Social and Preventive Medicine, vol. 49, no. 4, pp. 281-289

Savulescu, J.; Foddy, B. & Clayton, M. (2004): Why we should allow performance enhancing drugs in sport: The legalisation of drugs in sport may be fairer and safer. In: British Journal of Sports Medicine, vol. 38, no. 6, pp. 666-670, http://bjsm.bmj.com/content/38/6/666.full

Scheerder, J. & Van Tuyckom, C. (2007): Sportparticipatie in de Europese Unie. Vlaanderen vergeleken met her Europa van de 25. In: Scheerder, J.; Van Tuyckom, C. & Vermeersch, A. (eds): Europa in beweging. Sport vanuit Europees perspectief. Ghent: Academia Press, pp. 123-157

Schimank, U. (2006): Differenzierung und Integration der modernen Gesellschaft. Beiträge zur akteurzentrierten Differenzierungstheorie 1. Wiesbaden: VS Verlag für Sozialwissenschaften

Schmid, C. & Bojack, B. (2008): Soziale Ursachen der Adipositas bei Kindern und Jugendlichen und ihre Bedeutung für die sozialen Hilfen. In: Theorie und Praxis der Sozialen Arbeit, vol. 59, no. 3, pp. 179-185

Schön, D. (1983): The Reflective Practitioner. How professionals think in action, London: Temple Smith

Sjöström, M.; Oja, P.; Hagströmer, M.; Smith, B.J. & Bauman, A. (2006): Health-enhancing physical activity across European Union countries: the Eurobarometer study. In: Journal of Public Health, vol. 14, no. 5, pp. 291-300

Smith, M.K. (1994) Local Education, Buckingham: Open University Press

Smith, M.K. (2001): Donald Schön: learning, reflection and change. In: the encyclopedia of informal education, www.infed.org/thinkers/et-schon.htm

Sobal, J. (1995): The medicalization and demedicalization of obesity. In Maurer, D. and Sobal, J. (eds) Eating Agendas: Food and Nutrition as Social Problems. New York: Aldine de Gruyter., pp. 67-90

Subiotto, R. (2010): The adoption and enforcement of anti-doping rules should not be subject to European competition law. In: European Competition Law Review, vol. 31, no. 8, pp. 323-330

Szyszczak, E.; Bogusz, B. & Cygan, A. (eds) (2007): The Regulation of Sport in the European Union. Cheltenham: Edward Elgar

Teilmann Petersen, A. (2008): Fede tider. Hvordan bliver bekæmpelse af overvægt en opgave for pædagogikken? In: Dansk pædagogisk Tidsskrift, vol. 2008, no. 3, pp. 82-89

Teuffel, F. (2010): Die Dopingbekämpfung kommt nicht von der Stelle. Die Nationale Anti-Doping-Agentur hat in drei Jahren drei Geschäftsführer verloren. Es scheint nicht attraktiv zu sein, für die Nada zu arbeiten. Ein Kommentar. In: Die Zeit, 28.09.2010 - 10:00 Uhr. http://www.zeit.de/sport/2010-09/nada-ruecktritt-wewer

Thomas, W.I. & Thomas, D.S. (1928): The Child in America: Behavior Problems and Programs. New York, NY: Knopf

T.M.C. Asser Instituut (2010): The implementation of the WADA Code in the European Union. Report commissioned by the Flemish Minister responsible for Sport in view of the Belgian Presidency of the European Union in the second half of 2010. The Hague: T.M.C. Asser Instituut.
http://www.asser.nl/upload/documents/9202010_100013rapport%20Asserstudie%20(Engels).pdf

TNS Opinion & Social (2004): Special Eurobarometer 213 / Wave 62.0: The citizens of the European Union and Sport. Brussels: European Commission.
http://ec.europa.eu/public_opinion/archives/ebs/ebs_213_summ_en.pdf

TNS Opinion & Social (2010): Special Eurobarometer 334 / Wave 72.3: Sport and Physical Activity. Brussels: European Commission.
http://ec.europa.eu/public_opinion/archives/ebs/ebs_334_en.pdf

Todd, O. (2005): André Malraux: A Life. New York: Knop

Tokarski, W.; Petry, K.; Groll, M. & Mittag, J. (2009): A Perfect Match? Sport and the European Union. Aachen: Meyer & Meyer

Tokarski, W. & Steinbach, D. (2001): Spuren. Sportpolitik und Sportstrukturen in der Europäischen Union. Aachen: Meyer & Meyer

Tokarski, W.; Steinbach, D.; Petry, K. & Jesse, B. (2004): Two Players – One Goal? Sport in the European Union. Aachen: Meyer & Meyer

Troiano, R. & Haskell, W.L. (2010): The Role of Physical Activity Guidelines in Preventing Physical Inactivity. In: Brown, W.J.; Havas, E. & Komi, P.V. (eds): Promoting Sport for All: Benefits and Strategies for the 21st Century. Jyväskylä, Finland: 13th World Sport for All Congress 14-17th June 2010, pp. 33-39

Tzormpatzakis, N. & Sleap, M. (2007): Participation in physical activity and exercise in Greece: a systematic literature review. In: International Journal of Public Health, vol. 52, pp. 360-371

UBE [European Basketball Players' Union] (2009): Final Technical Report VS/2008/0271 Study on the working conditions of Professional basketball players in the European Union. Supported by a grant from the European Commission. Bologna: UBE

Van den Bogaert, S. (2010): Bosman: The Genesis of European Sports Law, The Past and Future of EU Law. In: Poiares Maduro, M.P. & Azoulai, L. (Hrsg.) (2010): The Classics of EU Law Revisited on the 50th Anniversary of the Rome Treaty 2010. Oxford & Portland, Oregon: Hart Publishing, pp. 488-497

van Schendelen, M.P.C.M. (2006): Machiavelli in Brussels. Amsterdam University Press

Vermeersch, A. (2006): The European Union and the Fight against Doping in Sport: on the field or on the sidelines? In: Entertainment and Sports Law Journal, vol. 4, no. 1, http://go.warwick.ac.uk/eslj/issues/volume4/number1/vermeersch

Vest Christiansen, A. (2006): "A Clean Amateur Makes a Good Professional": deviance, professionalism and doping in Danish cycling. In: Spitzer, G. (ed): Doping and Doping Control in Europe. Aachen: Meyer & Meyer, pp. 168-181

Vieweg, K. & Siekmann, R. (Hrsg.) (2007): Legal Comparison and the Harmonisation of Doping Rules. Pilot Study für die European Commission. Berlin: Duncker & Humblot

Voigt, B. (2010): Nach dem Prozess ist vor dem Prozess. Claudia Pechstein läuft Gefahr, nicht wegen ihrer Erfolge, sondern als Querulantin in die Sportgeschichte einzugehen. Benedikt Voigt ist von diesem Dopingfall genervt. In: Die Zeit, 27.01.2010 - 09:52 Uhr, http://www.zeit.de/sport/2010-01/pechstein-doping-eilantrag-olympia

WADA [World Anti Doping Agency] (2009a): International Standard for the Protection of Privacy and Personal Information (ISPPPI). June 2009. http://www.wada-ama.org/Documents/World_Anti-Doping_Program/WADP-IS-PPPI/ WADA_IS_PPPI_2009_EN.pdf

WADA [World Anti Doping Agency] (2009b): World Anti-Doping Code 2009. http://www.wada-ama.org/rtecontent/document/code_v2009_En.pdf

Wadden, T.A.; Vogt, R.A.; Anderson, R.E.; Bartlett, S.J.; Foster, G.D., Kuehnel, R.H., et al. (1997): Exercise in the treatment of obesity: Effects of four interventions on body composition, resting energy expenditure, appetite, and mood. In: Journal of Consulting and Clinical Psychology, vol. 65, pp. 269-277

Waddington, I. (2010): Surveillance and control in sport: a sociologist looks at the WADA whereabouts system. In: International Journal of Sport Policy and Politics, vol. 2, no.3, pp. 255-274

Walker, N. (2010): Open or Closure? The Constitutional Intimations of the ECJ. In: Poiares Maduro, M. & Azoulai, L. (eds) (2010): The Past and Future of EU Law. The Classics of EU Law Revisited on the 50th Anniversary of the Rome Treaty. Oxford & Portland, Oregon: Hart Publishing, pp. 333-342

Walker, S. (2009): Obesity Errors. In: Professional Social Work: Magazine of the British Association of Social Workers (BASW), March, p. 10

Watson, P. (2010): The German Genius. Europe's Third Renaissance, the Second Scientific Revolution, and the Twentieth Century. New York: Harper

Weatherill, S. (2003): Fair Play Please! Recent developments in the application of EC law to sport. In: Common Market Law Review, J. 40, H. 1, S. 51-93

Weatherill, S. (2010): Bosman Changed Everything: The Rise of EC Sports Law, the Past and Future of EU Law. In: Poiares Maduro, M.P. & Azoulai, L. (eds): The Classics of EU Law Revisited on the 50th Anniversary of the Rome Treaty 2010. Oxford & Portland, Oregon: Hart Publishing, pp.480-487

Wedderkopp, N.; Andersen, L.B.; Hansen, H.S. & Froberg, K. (2001). Fedme blandt børn – med særlig vægt på danske forhold. In: Ugeskrift for Læger, vol. 163, pp. 2907-2912

Weed, M.; Coren, E.; Fiore, J.; Mansfield, L.; Wellard, I.; Chatziefstathiou, D. & Dowse, S. (2009): A Systematic Review of the Evidence Base for Developing a Physical Activity and Health Legacy from the London 2012 Olympic and Paralympic Games. http://www.london.nhs.uk/publications/independent-publications/independent-reports/a-systematic-review-of-the-evidence-base-for-developing-a-phsyical-activity-and-health-legacy-from-the-london-2012-olympic-and-paralympic-games

WHO [World Health Organisation] (2006): Fact sheet N°311. September 2006. Obesity and overweight: What are overweight and obesity? http://www.who.int/mediacentre/factsheets/fs311/en/index.html

WHO [World Health Organisation] (2006a): European Charter on counteracting obesity. WHO European Ministerial Conference on Counteracting Obesity (Istanbul, Turkey, 15–17 November 2006), EUR/06/5062700/8. 16 November 2006. http://www.euro.who.int/__data/assets/pdf_file/0009/87462/E89567.pdf

Wong, Y.L.R. & Vinsky, J. (2009): Speaking from the Margins: A Critical Reflection on the 'Spiritual-but-not-Religious' Discourse in Social Work. In: British Journal of Social Work, vol. 39, pp. 1343-1359